SILENCED

SILENCED

With A New Introduction

Makeda Silvera

Talks with working class Caribbean women
about their lives and struggles as
Domestic Workers in Canada

Sister Vision
Black Women and Women of Colour Press

ISBN 0-920813-73-9

Seventh Printing 2000
The revised edition of *Silenced* was first published by Sister Vision: Black
Women and Women of Colour Press, Canada in 1989 — Fourth Printing.
Silenced was first published by Williams-Wallace Publishers Inc., Canada
in 1983.

00 01 02 03 04 ML 10-9-8-7
Printed and bound in Canada

Canadian Cataloguing in Publication Data

Main entry under title:
Silvera, Makeda, 1955 -
Silenced

Revised with new introduction.
Includes bibliographical references.

ISBN 0-920813-73-9

1. Women Domestics - Canada - Case studies.
2. Women, Black - West Indies. I. Title

HD6072.2.C3S55   1989   305.4'364   C89-095457-7

*Sister Vision Press acknowledges the financial support of the Canada
Council and the Ontario Arts Council toward its publishing program.*

Represented in Canada by Kate Walker & Company Ltd
Distributed in Canada and the United States
by The University of Toronto Press

Published by:
SISTER VISION
Black Women and Women of Colour Press
P.O. Box 217, Station E
Toronto, Ontario
Canada M6H 4E2
(416) 533-9353
E-mail: sisvis@web.net

This book is dedicated to my grandmother Lucille May Johnson, a Jamaican working class woman of a very striking and compassionate personality. And to the women in this book, with much love.

Introduction to the Second Edition

This new introduction comes six years after the first publication of *Silenced* in 1983. The book was an immediate success and between 1983 and 1988 it was reprinted three times. It was the first of its kind; that is, the first account in Canadian history of Caribbean domestic workers talking about their work experiences and living conditions in Canada.

New introductions are supposed to introduce new findings, to update and shed new light on the subject of study, but the single most important statement that this new introduction can make is that there is nothing new; were this book written today about the collective experience of the women, their voices would say the same thing because the situation has changed minimally since the first publication of *Silenced*. For example in 1983 domestic workers on the work permit earned $3.50 per hour, in 1989, they earn $5.00 per hour. They are entitled to work no more than 44 hours per week, beyond that they are entitled to time and a half. They can now register complaints with the Ministry of Labour to claim for overtime wages if their employers refuse to acknowledge this. For many domestic workers, this entitlement is seen as bureaucratic jargon, the reality remains the same as it was in 1983, and that is, individual women remain afraid and intimidated and complaints of any kind are rarely registered. The perception of domestic work and those who work as domestics have not changed, nor the reasons for coming to Canada to do this kind of work.

Yet despite this sense of frustrating stagnation, this new introduction offers reflective analysis of the historical/political climate in Toronto during the early and late 1970's; for it is the climate experienced by the Black community which helped set the stage for a book like *Silenced*. This new introduction, provides, also a further opportunity to discuss the process of writing the book and the importance of using oral history as a methodology to chart the experiences of Caribbean domestic workers.

The 1970's signalled both the birth and simultaneous coming of age of the Black community. The community built on the struggles of previous generations who in organizations like the Universal African Improvement Association (UAIA), The Negro Citizenship Association, the Canadian Negro Women's Association, and with individuals like Harry Gairey, Don Moore, Violet Blackman, Carrie Best, fought the earlier battles for dignity and justice. In the 1970's the demographic expansion of the community facilitated the emergence and development of new talents, new organizations, new strategies. Much of this activism in Toronto's Black community was spearheaded by the student movement.

In responding to the political situation of Blacks in Canada we were encouraged by our brothers and sisters south of the border, who were demanding equal rights and justice for Blacks in the United States. The situation demanded re-active and pro-active strategies and the community responded with numerous groups, committees, organizations which sought to confront the issues. The issues were numerous: discrimination in housing and employment, undeniable institutional bias in education, increasing police abuse of authority and official harassment characterised by the random deportation of racially visible groups. Many Caribbean domestic workers were affected by all of these issues and in particular by random deportation. Although because of their legal status they were only tenuously connected to the wider Black community our plight was theirs and their struggle for dignity ours.

The Black community newspaper often reported the heart-rending situations of some of these domestics, yet in retrospect it seemed as if there was no time for activists to record and to document this important and historic period for posterity. Many activists and leaders who participated in the political movements did not seem to realize how important it was to document and chronicle that period of history. My decision to work on *Silenced* was clearly informed by this gap in our cultural development. It became increasingly clearer to me that as the community matured and grew in strength, it required some kind of documentation of its past, which would inform its present and be available for future generations in their struggle. The task of recording the total picture, that is, the struggles of the wider community appeared overwhelming and to some extent remote. But because of my direct involvement in grassroots activism and my years of involvement in organizing and working with Caribbean domestic workers I took on the challenge of recording their experiences.

In 1977 I was working as a journalist for *Contrast* (a Black newspaper) and I was assigned to cover a demonstration which was in support of seven Jamaican women who were facing deportation by the Canadian government. The case was dubbed 'The Seven Jamaican Mothers' although in fact there were more than seven women who were facing deportation. Many of these women had come to Canada in the early 1970's to work as domestics as part of a Jamaica-Canada agreement similar to the domestic scheme of 1955. Both arrangements sought to transfer surplus labour from stagnant Caribbean countries to satisfy the need for cheap domestic labour in an expanding Canadian economy. One of the 'qualifications' for this kind of job was that the woman had to be single and without children.

Many of the women claimed that on the advice of the Jamaican government and with the knowledge of the Canadian High Commission staff they omitted on their application forms the fact that they had children. Many of these women worked for years as domestics in Canada. Some had been in Canada since 1971 and had applied for landed status and received it. In 1975, the government arbitrarily decided to deport many of these women who had been granted landed status. The charge was that they had submitted fake immigration applications claiming they had no children, but were now attempting to apply for landed status for children they now acknowledged in Jamaica.

This was clearly sexist since single fathers were not routinely rounded up and deported. In fact men were never asked about children. It was also clearly racist because it was only Black landed immigrants who were being deported. There were no known cases of non-black women who were harassed and deported during that period. It was only Caribbean women who, forced to emigrate as domestics as part of their strategy for economic survival, had to deny the existence of their children and were now paying for this indiscretion.

The attack against domestics had to be understood against a background of changing economic conditions in Canada and the consequent changing need for imported cheap labour. It was in the late 1970's when the Canadian economic picture had changed and local unemployment had risen to a new high that the government began to round up these women on charges of fraud. Many felt that the intent of the government was to intimidate these women and to send them home now that their services were no longer needed. It was the general opinion that this attack on domestics was part of a policy to appease those uninformed Canadians who erroneously believed that Black immigrants were denying jobs to the unemployed.

During the next two years while the women and their supporters continued to battle against the racist and sexist policy of Canadian immigration department, I came to know and work with many of these women. We demonstrated in the harsh Canadian winter, we cried together and when we finally won we rejoiced together. I was touched deeply by their lives of struggle and whatever personal problems I had, seemed trivial in the face of their continual struggle for respect.

The success of the Seven Jamaican Mothers and their victory was in large measures due to many of them speaking for the first time at large rallies about their plight, the wide media coverage their case received and the public outcry from many Canadians. There were numerous demonstrations organized so that the general public could be sensitized to the plight of these women. The case was fought on many different levels, through mass organizing, media report, demonstrations, leafletting, press conferences and in the courts. It was clear that the case could not be won only in the court room. It required the active participation and agitation of supporters who demonstrated, picketed and signed petitions. The plight of these unprotected domestics evoked responses from many organizations both within the Black community and other non-black progressive groups. These organizations and groups included The International Committee Against Racism, Canadians Against the Deportation of Immigrant Women, the Universal African Improvement Association, the Canadian Labour Party, teachers, trade unionists, church leaders, and the Sikh community. It was difficult for any government to ignore this widely based ground swell of opposition to this inhumane and discriminatory policy.

ORAL HISTORY AS METHODOLOGY

Oral history is the lifeline of this book. It is a book about women talking directly to the reader about their lives and their experiences. It is a powerful and a living testimony of the voices of 'the ordinary' and the 'powerless'. Oral historians can learn from these testimonies because the document bring into the forefront the lived experience of the voiceless. It forces one to confront the imposed muteness which has silenced women for so long and it encourages the recognition of the revolutionary potential of women's oral history. As a Black feminist engaged in research I have become more aware of the neglect of the contributions to the Canadian society of peoples of colour and in particular Black women. This oral documentation fills the gap in Canadian herstory and attempts to satisfy the need for a reference text that relates the politics of Caribbean domestic workers.

In 1980 when I began work on Caribbean domestic workers in Canada, I was relatively new to academia and to feminist research. But I was both optimistic and enthusiastic about beginning work in this area. Two things struck me: one that there was little significant research in this area and consequently an absence of empirical data, and two, that the existing material was for the most part clinical, and devoid of a life or rhythm of the 'subject'. The only available work that provided a feel of the reality of the life of Caribbean domestics in Canada were the novels by West Indian author Austin Clarke. I wanted to find a sociological work that was similar to Clarke's novels. I wanted to find a herstory of Caribbean women that was real - a piece of work in the voices of the women. It was reading other oral herstories of working class women written mostly in the United States and examining the oral research of Black historians in the United States that established for me the value of oral history as a methodology.

One of the most striking and obvious things about *Silenced* is the use of language by the ten women. They speak in their own words, in their own language, filled with all the cultural nuances and innuendos. This is an act of empowerment, particularly for these women who work as live-in domestics and for the most part have not been able to speak in their own language on a daily basis but have had to speak in another 'language' to communicate with their employer. Language is a powerful aspect of culture. When it is taken away from an individual, it is an act of disempowering that person. How does this affect them? How do they maintain family ties and traditions?

The traditional methodological instruments of the academic are inadequate to handle the complexities of recognizing the extent of powerlessness and engaging in the task of empowerment. Perhaps in their defense it may be said that they were not designed for the task of engaged scholarship which is the mandate of the committed feminist scholar especially from the Third World. The questionnaire, the survey, have their value/role/importance for those who from a distance attempt what is described by some as disinterested and dispassionate observation and analysis. I have no quarrel with that. But my mandate is different. My task is not merely to observe and record, but it is to facilitate that entry into public scrutiny those who must be the makers of their own history rather than merely the subjects of the recorders of history. Yet this task is not without its own 'rules', methodological dangers; the oral historian must be familiar with the langauge and other aspects of the culture. The interviewer should be aware of cultural taboos and customs. Unfamiliarity with the language and cultural sensibilities can seriously affect the content of the interview. By this I mean that it is important to know what areas are taboo in a particular cultural context. For example a woman might discuss with the interviewer the number of children she has and her children's fathers. Depending on the degree of privacy she wishes to maintain, she might become silent if you then proceed to ask her about her marital status. This might well be an open secret, something she talks freely about to her friends, but face to face in an interview she might want to eliminate this point.

What I would like to get back to and to single out for some discussion is the interview process. When I started work on *Silenced*, I was curious about the protocol for interviewing. I found there were not many examples available which spoke directly about interviewing women, or with a 'female sensibility'. The reference books spoke about appearing neutral in an interview, not give any opinions, being professional and cool, being in control and not sharing information about self to the interviewee. In the book *Methods in Social Research*, Goode and Hatt maintained:

> Consequently, the interviewer cannot merely lose himself in being friendly. He must introduce himself as though beginning a conversation but from the beginning the additional element of respect, of professional competence, should be maintained. Even the beginning student will make this attempt, else he will find himself merely

'maintaining rapport', while failing to penetrate the cliches of contradictions of the respondent. Further he will find that his own confidence is lessened, if the only goal is to maintain friendliness. He is a professional researcher in this situation and he must demand and obtain respect for the task he is trying to perform.[1] (pg.191)
(A. Oakley, "Interviewing women", as cited in H. Roberts (ed)
Doing Feminist Research)

C.A. Moser, talks about the problems of becoming too talkative with the interviewee.

Some interviewers are no doubt better than others at establishing what the psychologists call 'rapport' and some may even be too good at it - the National Opinion Research Centre Studies found slightly less satisfactory results from the ... sociable interviewers who are 'fascinated by people' ... there is something to be said for the interviewer who, while friendly and interested does not get too emotionally involved with the respondent and his problems.... Pleasantness and a business-like nature is the ideal combination.[2] (pp.l87-8, 195)
(A. Oakley, "Interviewing women", as cited in H. Roberts (ed)
Doing Feminist Research)

It is clear from the techniques suggested here that the interviewer must be duplicitous and that this formal deception ostensibly in the pursuit of distance, or disinterestedness is a stock in trade of the interview. But perhaps this may be a male-centred approach. I suggest that in interviewing women we may require less distance and more openness.
Let me state clearly, that in any situation where one is the interviewer, a power dynamic already exists. The interviewer's knowledge of this and sensitivity around this issue is important. It is the sharing of information about self, as much as that is possible, that breaks the dominant/dominated dynamic. As feminists working in this area we have a responsibility to break down these traditional male dominant ways of research and replace them with ones that speak to us from the standpoint of women.

The kind of interviewing techniques suggested, would not have resulted in a book like *Silenced*. The very act of asking women to speak for themselves, makes it clear that the interviewer has an opinion, that we are interested in their lives and that we are departing from the traditional male-centred ways of interviewing.

There are vast numbers of topics and issue that can be explored through oral history, which would continue to build on the precious little documentation available on Black women. They include among others Caribbean women and ageing in Canada; young Black women who migrated to

Canada as teenagers; recounting our grandmothers' lives; Black immigrants who came here in the 1940's; and there is still more work to be done on domestic labour.

Though, private, hidden, and regarded as unimportant it is a everyday experience of women, and who better to speak, who better to listen to, who better to learn from, but the women themselves, and in this case domestic workers. They can provide insight into the support network which operates in domestic workers circles, the sexual exploitation of domestics, their affiliation with the church, concerns around ageing and their vision and hope for a better future.

These oral herstories with Caribbean domestic workers uncover a wealth of information about migration, about class, race and gender, and present to us much information that has not been previously recorded. These interviews show clearly that Caribbean domestic workers have played and are playing an important historical role in Canadian economic development as cheap labour to fill Canada's labour shortage.

Makeda Silvera
September 1989

Table of Contents

Acknowledgements

I am profoundly grateful to the women whose collective decision to be Silenced no longer are the heart-beat of this book. They participated in this collective process with strength, warmth and gave unselfishly of their time to make this book a reality. I thank them all for trusting me, for sharing their lives and for their friendship. I would have liked to list each and every one of these women's names on this page, but they are on the Temporary Employment Visa and their names must not be mentioned for fear of harassment and deportation.

For helping me to meet some of the women in this book, Molly — who is on the Temporary Employment Visa — and also Eva Smith, a former domestic worker, who is now a community worker and who gave unselfishly of her time in the organisation of the Domestic Workers Group.

I especially want to thank and express my gratitude to Lois DeShield of the Immigrant Women's Job Placement Centre who, in a very special way, helped to make this book possible.

I am also deeply grateful to Patricia K. Murphy; as an editor and a friend she made a valuable contribution to this book. She has seen the book through each successive version and has helped in sharpening its vision and expression. For this I cannot say sufficient thanks.

To Dr. David Trotman who read/criticised and encouraged this project.

To Bromley Armstrong of the Ontario Labour Relations Board who shared with me his knowledge of the Ontario Black communities in the early 1940's and 50's.

To Pamela Godfree, the whiz at the typesetting machine, for her speed and accuracy.

To Susan Sturman for her help with paste-up.

My special thanks to Sheila Block who proofread everything and spent weekends and nights double proofing the boards. Also, Nila Gupta and Doug Stewart for their help with proofreading.

To Erica Mercer, Filomena Carvalho and the staff of the Immigrant Women's Centre for their support throughout the project.

To Himani Bannerji and Lin Delaney who helped me to understand the difference between 'being silent' and 'being silenced'.

To Stephanie Martin who believes, advises, consoles and is always there with words of encouragement.

Finally, a great big thanks to all my friends who believed in this project.

Introduction to the First Edition

This is a book about the lives and struggles of West Indian women who are employed as domestic workers on Temporary Employment Visas in Canada. In it, ten women tell of their day to day struggles as Black working class women.

The women in the book come from the English-speaking Caribbean. Some of the women are from Jamaica while the others are from Trinidad, St. Vincent, Antigua, St. Lucia and Guyana. All of them have children who are left in the care of grandmothers or other relatives back home. These women came to Canada to work as domestic workers with the hopes that they will make enough money to feed, clothe and educate their families back in the Caribbean.

> When I first came to this country, I came with three intentions — to help my kids, to go to school, to better myself, and to go to work and save some money. But now that I'm here, I find can neither save money, go to school or send for your kids.[1]

The misconception of Canada as the land of milk and honey is reinforced by airline advertisements, domestic agencies, weekly dramas on the television set which show North America as the land of plenty where happiness and wealth can be bought on credit and where maids like those shown on the weekly sit-coms, are treated with respect and as a special part of the family.

What is never talked about, or made clear to many of these women is the widespread prejudice they will come up against in Canada and the racism imbedded within a system which thrives on the labour of women of colour from Third World countries, women who are brought to Canada to work virtually as legal slaves in the homes of both wealthy and middle class Canadian families. In most cases both their employers are themselves employed and have an average combined income of $40,000 to $100,000 a year. Meanwhile, women who work in these homes as domestic servants get as little as $200 a month for an eighteen hour day, seven days a week job.

> Right now my day begins at round 5 a.m. ... sometimes after 7 p.m. you want to put on your sleep clothes, but it is not possible because sometimes at 10 p.m. they calling you to feed the eight month-old baby if he wake up. Then when the children sick, when they have the cold, it's me who have to get up, not their mother and father.[2]

The recruitment of female immigration labour for upper and middle class Canadian families from outside of Canada was, and remains the most effective means used for securing domestic labour. In the book *Women at Work (Ontario 1850-1930): Domestic Service in Canada*, Genevieve Leslie discusses this briefly.

> In 1911, for example, immigrant women formed thirty-five per cent of the female work force in domestic and personal service, even though they made up only twenty-four per cent of the female work force in all occupations including service jobs. Female domestics were "preferred immigrants" long before 1880 but the drive to recruit immigrant domestics intensified as industrialization diverted (Canadian) women from service into other occupations.[3]

Many of these women were poor and came from families who could no longer support them; others were homeless and some were in fact children from workhouses in Britain.

> The usual arrangement was that an employer applied for a servant and sent her passage money to the Superintendent of Immigration. An immigration agent would then choose a domestic in the Old Country, have her sign an agreement which bound her to service with her employer from six months to a year, advance her passage money, and arrange for her transportation, housing, and placement upon arrival. The amount advanced would later be deducted from the domestic's salary in monthly installments. [4]

On the job, they encountered many of the same problems that today's live-in domestic workers face, including sexual harassment, long hours and low pay. The general pattern of these immigrant women was that as soon as they completed their tenure agreement, they left domestic work and went on to other jobs with better working conditions.

An immigrant domestic complained in 1919 that the agent in London (England)....

> Has so much to say about the good time maids have and how free you are, that you decide you will come.... The lady meets you at Union Station, takes you to her house, where she has employers waiting to engage you. You have no choice of a place or work — just have to go where you are sent. [5]

There was a high turnover rate, since European immigrant women and girls did not stay long in these jobs. Because of this, the Canadian government attempted to take a look at some of the problems of this special group of women and became more involved in the recruitment of domestic servants from abroad.

In 1898, for example, a Mrs. Livingstone was commissioned by the Department of the Interior to travel to Scotland and select one hundred girls for service in the North West. Mrs. Livingstone attempted to match servant and employer when choosing women for immigration, by allowing servants to evaluate employers and decide where they would like to work — "actually realising the oft laughed at idea of the kitchen demanding that the drawing room, like it, should give references." However, this arrangement was considered troublesome. It was soon discarded, while employers continued to specify age, physique, race, character and experience of the servants they wanted. [6]

The problems between employer and employee continued, particularly in the case of the live-in domestic worker, who was on call twenty-four hours a day. As tenure was completed hundreds of women left domestic work. Many sought jobs in factories, dress shops and offices. These women quickly assimilated into the Canadian society.

As the need for domestic workers grew, Canada began to look at Third World countries to supply domestic labour.

The first full-scale recruitment of West Indian women to Canada was initiated in 1955 by the Canadian government. These women came under a new organised program, known then, as The Domestic Scheme. Hundreds of women from Jamaica, Trinidad and Barbados came to Canada annually to work as domestic workers through this Scheme.

To qualify for the Scheme, applicants had to be between the ages of eighteen and thirty-five, single, with at least a grade eight education, and be able to pass a medical examination. Final applicants were interviewed by a team of Canadian immigration officials who visited the islands once a year specifically for this purpose. [7]

Many of these women were sole-support mothers. Upon arriving in Canada, they were granted landed immigrant status, and like their European sisters before them, they were required to work in a home for a period of one year. After a year's service, they had the option of finding work in another field or remaining in domestic labour.

Not much has been documented about this group of workers. "Hearsay and rumour stress the alienation and loneliness of these women and their difficulties in assimilating to the new Canadian scene."[8] But what is well known, though, is that like their European counterparts, they too found domestic work unrewarding, the hours long and the salary inadequate. They too, eventually left domestic work after their contracts had expired. Many went back to school to upgrade their education and move on to better jobs, but unlike European women, many Caribbean women experienced downward mobility, and because of their colour and the racism they experienced, found it much harder to assimilate into the larger society. This did not stop the determination of many Caribbean women who opted out of domestic work after their tenure was completed; because of this pattern, the shortage of domestic workers continued to increase. The department of Employment and Immigration appeared not to be interested in improving the situation of many West Indians who decided to abandon domestic work. Instead of taking steps to improve the working conditions of domestic workers, the government stopped granting automatic landed immigrant status to domestics, thus putting an end to the Domestic Scheme, and instead issued Temporary Employment Visas.

TEMPORARY EMPLOYMENT VISAS

Temporary Employment Visas are, for the most part, issued to workers from Third World countries. The main purpose of the Temporary Employment Visa is to fill the labour shortage in certain jobs inside Canada, in particular, domestic labour, seasonal farmwork and other non-union jobs, where the wages are rock-bottom and the working conditions reminiscent of the 19th century. Each visa is issued for a particular kind of job, for a specific employer and for a definite period of time. If any of these circumstances change, the holder of a visa must immediately report to the Employment and Immigration Commission or run the risk of being deported.

Unlike the Domestic Scheme of 1955 and the others before, the holder of a Temporary Employment Visa is not automatically entitled to landed immigrant status. The Canadian Employment and Immigration Commission considers employment visas a "temporary solution" to the domestic labour shortage, and thus feels quite justified in exploiting the labour of Third World women and turning a blind eye to the inhumane working conditions that have become synonymous with domestic work.

In *Union Sisters* (The Women's Press, Toronto 1983), Rachel Epstein confirms the excessive use of cheap immigrant labour, with figures obtained from Employment and Immigration Canada. She argues that:

> In 1974 the number of landed immigrants admitted to Canada was
> two and a half times as great as the number of employment visas
> issued. In 1978 the balance was reversed and there were more visas
> issued than landed immigrants admitted. Although in 1981 the numbers
> were almost equal, this represented a substantial increase in the
> numbers of people entering the country on employment visas and a
> decrease in the numbers of landed immigrants from previous years.[9]

In 1978, 12,483 Temporary Employment Visas were issued for domestic work in Canada. The bulk of these were issued in Ontario, Quebec, British Columbia and Alberta. In 1982, there were more than 16,000 visas issued, despite the fact that unemployment in Canada had been rising at an alarming rate.

The major reason for this increase in Temporary Employment Visas is that few Canadian workers are willing to do this work, which requires, in most cases, 'living-in'.

LIVING AND WORKING CONDITIONS

The living and working conditions of employment visa holders differs from home to home, depending on the individual employer, but in general, the working conditions are poor and in some cases totally unacceptable.

Employment and Immigration Canada has established certain minimum standards to be used as guidelines by people who employ workers on the Temporary Employment Visas. According to Employment and Immigration, the worker should receive $710.00 per month (in Ontario), with a deduction of $210.00 per month for room and board. The worker must also pay Unemployment Insurance and Canada Pension. The guidelines also state that the domestic's working period is an eight hour day and provides for two days off each week.

The reality for domestic workers differs greatly from these depart-mental regulations. On the contrary, what is most common is that the employer does not follow these guidelines. Many employers view these guidelines as a mere bureaucratic formality. They have, in fact, a free hand in setting wages because Immigration does little to enforce its regulations. So, duties, hours of work and salaries are often changed unilaterally by the employer. One worker complains:

> The other day I was telling a friend of mine about Mrs. Smith and the meagre salary she was paying me. My friend was asking how she manage to get away with it from Manpower. But the thing is, Manpower don't know because she told Manpower she was paying me $100.00 a week. It's on the paper. It's written down in the contract ... when I started working with her she told me she was paying me $85.00 a week. [10]

The Employment and Immigration Commission advises that if an employer does not adhere to these rules, the employee should contact a Canada Employment and Immigration Centre, where an officer will assist the permit holder in finding another job as a domestic. But there is a huge gap between stated policy and the real experience. Therefore, many women when faced with a breach of contract are afraid to make a formal complaint to an Immigration officer.

> Right now I get $710.00 a month, which is what I am suppose to get as Manpower say, but when I took the job, I wasn't told that I was suppose to clean and wash clothes too for that money. I am afraid to go and complain to Manpower, because this is my third job... so maybe if I go and complain they might tell me to go home. They might think I am a troublemaker. [11]

These sentiments are the norm. Employment visa holders who have had more than one employer have been forced to leave the country by Immigration officers. Many of the women in this book do not get two days off each week as stipulated in their contracts. Some are not even aware that they are entitled to statutory holidays. Many of the women complain that they must share their rooms with the younger children or babies in the family. Others reported that they were not given enough food, despite the fact that employers deduct money for room and board. Domestic workers also receive no overtime or vacation pay. They are not covered under the Canada Pension Plan and cannot collect Unemployment Insurance even though they pay into it. As stated earlier, the Employment and Immigration Commission has made attempts to set up some minimum standards for wages and working conditions, but have done nothing about employers who renege on their agreement. This policy clearly benefits certain sectors of Canadian society, by supplying substantial amounts of cheap imported labour to fill the domestic needs of upper and middle class Canadian families. It is also an effective way of controlling the permanent migration of Third World working class women to Canada.

EDUCATIONAL OPPORTUNITIES

Up until recently, women on the employment visa were prohibited by law from upgrading their education in Canada. Many of these women had been here for over nine years, working as live-in workers, paying into Unemployment Insurance and the Canada Pension Plan without having the right to vote and choose government representatives.

In the winter of 1980, a series of incidents concerning domestic workers on employment visas began to crop up in the media. One such incident that was widely reported was that of a domestic worker who took an Ontario Government minister to court for back wages.

There were countless other incidents that did not make the headlines or the 10 o'clock news, but which have been documented by community groups working with domestics. Many other cases appeared in court and through support of various community organisations, some women have been able to win their cases and collect their back-pay. If it had been the intention of the established newspapers and the government in power to ignore the demands of these women for justice, it was in vain.

In November 1981, the government was forced to look at its Immigration policy concerning domestic workers on the Temporary Employment Visa:

> Ottawa: Employment and Immigration Minister Lloyd Axworthy today announced new measures to assist foreign domestics working in Canada to gain permanent resident status...the measures follow an extensive review of the policy on domestic workers on the employment visa.[12]

Speaking about the change, the Minister said that domestic workers who have been in Canada for more than two years may apply for permanent resident status.

> Domestic workers currently in Canada who have been here two years, and who wish to be considered for permanent resident status, will be given the opportunity of gaining that status from within the country when their employment authorisations are due for renewal. Assessment will be made by Immigration officers, and those who have been here for two years and who have achieved a potential for self-sufficiency will be advised that they can make application for permanent resident status from within Canada. Those not yet sufficiently established or who have been here for less than two years will be given the opportunity for upgrading their skills to the point where they also can be considered for permanent resident status.[13]

But again, there is a gap between stated policy and practice. Though it is still too early to see the full implication of the new policy, one thing is certain and that is that it is much more complicated than it sounds. First, whether or not a woman qualifies for landed status is left up to the individual Immigration officer who must judge whether she has an "aptitude for learning," "an adaptability to Canadian lifestyle," and personal suitability." Given that there is no clear stated policy, this has already led to discriminatory practices. Already, older women who have been in Canada for nearly ten years, or women with more than four children are worried that their applications will be rejected.

The new policy also stipulated that Canadian employers must provide a certain amount of free time each week for domestic workers to attend upgrading courses at night school. The new policy also states that employers must contribute towards the cost of training during the time of study. But many employers are not providing the token $20.00 per month or the time off required. Again, and for obvious reasons, many women are afraid to bring this to the attention of Immigration officers.

THE WOMEN IN THIS BOOK

These women have never been heard. Usually we know of them through impersonalised cold statistics or through the voices of others who speak for them, or when the media sensationalises their plight and briefly force us to acknowledge, if only temporarily, that they exist.

I met most of the women in this book through my involvement in working with and helping to organise domestic workers. It was through my experience as a working class woman and my involvement with poor people that I developed the anger and persistence that pushed me forward to work on this book. And it was the warmth, and courage of these women that gave me the inspiration to complete it.

We rarely hear about women like Molly, Irma, Myrtle, Hyacinth or Angel, and when and if we do learn about their hopes, struggles and vision, it is often heard through the words of others. It is not their lack of education and lack of writing skills that have served to silence many of these women. It is rather that their silence is the result of a society which uses power and powerlessness as weapons to exclude non-white and poor people from any real decision-making and participation.

This book hopes to help to shatter this silence. Ten West Indian women talk about their lives as domestic workers in Canada, the bitter-sweet memories of family back home, the frustration of never having enough money and the humiliation of being a legal slave. They tell of working overtime for no pay, of sharing their rooms usually with a baby or the family pet, of shaking off the sexual advances of their male employer, and in the case of Hyacinth, of being raped. They talk about the experience of being manipulated and degraded by female employers. Although their cries are usually ones of despair at their isolation, they also talk about their lives as mothers and daughters and about continued visions of hope for the future.

Each chapter in this book represents a life story or a part of one. Their experiences illustrate a wide range of issues that concern them as workers and as women: sexual harassment, alienation, atrocious working and living conditions, inadequate pay, and inevitably, discrimination and oppression because of race, class and age.

All the women whose stories appear in this book are between the ages of twenty and fifty-four years old. Nine women are Black and one woman is East Indian from Guyana. All ten women are from poor and working class backgrounds. (This categorisation is based on their previous occupation in the Caribbean and their educational background.) Seven of the ten women did not attend high school, while three attended but did not complete it. Four of the ten women were unemployed in the Caribbean, five were employed as domestic workers, and one as a secretary. Nine of the ten women have children back home, and of that nine, seven are solely responsible for their children's financial welfare. Only one of the ten women is married and her husband remains in the Caribbean.

Although the interviews were generally unstructured, I approached them with a few specific topics that I was interested in — their views on the role of women, their views on feminism, and the relationship between their female employers and themselves. But after much thought about silence and the silenced, I felt that it was better to leave it at whatever each individual woman wanted to focus on. Since working class women do not often have the opportunity or the resources to write about their lives, it was important these women talk about whatever they wanted to, that they speak directly about the problems they face as domestic workers.

During the interviews, I respected each woman's decision on what were, for her, private areas. I did not want to drag painful memories out of people and then leave them to deal with the emotional aftermath alone. However, many of the women talked unabashedly and unguardedly, even about painful times. Some, like Molly, talked for hours on end; others cried in desperation and relief. Not one of us who participated were unmoved.

Although many of these women share the same feelings of loneliness, isolation and hope, they remain isolated from each other in suburban Canada, and will meet for the first time within the pages of this book.

Molly was one of the first persons I interviewed for the book. It was a very warm and intimate interview — the kind every interviewer dreams about. We sat down in her one room apartment and talked for five hours, taping the conversation as we talked.

A number of the women, particularly those who work as live-in domestics were interviewed at my house. These interviews followed much the same pattern as Molly's and were also taped.

Some interviews were easier than others. For example, when I first started to interview Primrose, I had a hard time trying to get her to talk about her feelings and her life in Canada as a domestic. It took a very long time to develop the trust that we now have. Nevertheless, it added an important sense of reality to our conversation, given the fear of many domestic workers of speaking out, the fear of being identified by their employers and, as a result, losing their jobs.

On the other hand, Angel's interview flowed quite smoothly and was very touching. She talked about her difficult relationship with her mother and the strains and anxieties that her mother also experienced as a domestic worker. But generally, the women were very eager to talk once trust and respect was established.

At the end of each interview, I took home the tapes, transcribed and then edited them. I then took the transcribed tapes back to the women, who read them over and sometimes suggested changes. Then I took them home again and re-typed them and gave them back to be read a final time.

If there were anxieties about parts of the interview, we talked it over and came to some amicable agreement. This was a very long and laborious process. The book took me three years to complete, juggled between my family, work, and academic and community activities. There were times when it was frustrating, and I felt like giving up, times when I didn't have enough money to buy tapes, to rent a typewriter, to buy paper or to pay for the other expenses that I incurred. At those times, I had to put the book on hold. Nonetheless, it was well worth the time and the money spent on typing and re-typing the manuscripts when the women wanted to change a paragraph or a page. I remember one woman being quite concerned about what she had said on tape about her family. She feared they might read the book and get angry with her. Upon reading the manuscript she felt that she had the power to change anything she wanted, and she did change it.

I hope that the lives and struggles of these women will provide other domestic workers with a sense of power and a sense of their own history.

I hope it will serve too, as a point of identity for all women who have been silenced. Here are ten stories of women who are silenced no longer. I say no more. Turn the pages and meet them.

Makeda Silvera
January 1983

Noreen

Sometimes when they can't get their own way they will call me 'nig', I know they mean nigger but I pretend I don't hear. I remember once I complain to their mother and she told me that I was too picky that they would grow out of it.

Noreen is a plump Black woman standing 5'4". Nearly fifty years old, she wears her short straightened black hair in a tight little bun. This and her thick-rimmed glasses make her appear much older than her forty-nine years.

Life has not been kind to Noreen and the deep, sharp lines that have set in on her face and neck are testimony to this.

Noreen is from the island of St. Vincent and has been in Canada on a work permit since 1977. She has never been back, nor has she seen any of her five children since she left the island.

Noreen lives with and works for a family of five in the Bathurst and Lawrence area. She earns $260.00 a month for a twenty-four hour, six-and-a-half day work week.

The first time I met Noreen was in the fall of 1981. I had taken my two children to the park to play on the swings when I noticed this sombre Black woman sitting on a park bench by herself. I went over and introduced myself to her and we started talking. I later found out that she was early for church services and was passing the time in the park.

We talked for what seemed like hours. She told me about her children, about St. Vincent and her life in Canada. She even gave me tips on a few home remedies for childhood ailments. All too soon we said goodbye, we exchanged numbers and promised to meet again in the park. We never did!

February 1982: My phone rings and it's Noreen. She's in the hospital with an ulcer.

I rushed down to see her, taking a bunch of flowers and a card. She asked me to keep her bank-book until after the operation and gave me the address of her daughter in St. Vincent whom I was to contact if there were any serious complications.

It was in May 1982 that I asked Noreen to be a part of this book. She pointedly said no. I told her I understood and we continued to talk about other things — back home, the winter, Canadian culture, children, grandchildren, etc. The next day I received a phone call from Noreen saying she'd do it. We made plans to meet the following Sunday afternoon at my house.

LIFE IN ST. VINCENT

"I was working as a day worker"

Before I came to Canada, I was working as a day worker in St. Vincent. I was getting about $30.00 a week, sometimes less, depending on how many houses I could clean in a week.

I have a cousin here who was working for a lady in Vancouver. She wrote to me and said the lady have a friend that was looking for a helper. I wrote to the lady and she write me back and outline that they wanted somebody to look after the house and take care of two children. She said that she and her husband would apply for me to come up on a work permit, that they would pay my way up and I could pay them back when I started working for them. It was a good break for me and I thank the Lord every day that he make it possible for me to leave St. Vincent. You know, it is very hard when you don't have the right education to get a good paying job when you have six mouths to feed.

I came up in 1977 and I am still with the same people that sponsored me up here. In the beginning, when I just came, things were rough for me, everything was so strange. I felt lonely and missed my children and country very much. Plus the people I live with were moving up and down.

"You begin to feel like a child, having to answer 'Yes Miss'"

When I first arrived in Vancouver, I have to admit I was a bit scared. I never see so much white people in one place from I born. Everywhere. I don't think I saw more than six Black people for the first eight months that I was in Vancouver. Everything was so different, it was like I was in another world.

The lady came to meet me at the airport with her husband. They had two little boys at the time. Now there is two more little boys in the family. I remember when they came to meet me in the airport, I was nervous. All the way home in the car I felt anxious. I remember on the way home in the car I had to keep saying "excuse me miss?," because they were talking so fast I couldn't understand. It took me a good year to feel a little comfortable. Not that the people treat me bad or anything, but you know after living in St. Vincent for forty-three years and coming here to work and live in somebody else house, you begin to feel like a child, having to answer "Yes miss" and on call all day and night. I still don't get used to that.

Sometimes after seven o'clock you want to put up your foot and relax, bathe and put on your sleep clothes, but it not possible because sometimes at ten o'clock they calling you to feed the eight-month-old baby if he wake up. Then when the children sick, when they have the cold, it's me who have to get up not their mother and father. Lord, sometimes I wonder when it going to end, I don't know, I leave it in the hands of the good Lord. I long for the day when I can sleep till nine or ten o'clock one morning, but you know I don't really complain because if I was back home, I couldn't help out my children with money and so on.

Like I said, the people don't treat me unkind, but sometimes the missis in a bad mood after work and she take it out on me, shout at me, and want to know what I do the whole day.

You know how housework is; you could tidy up the house and wash the dishes twenty times a day. At the end of the day, especially with three growing boy child, the house look like a hurricane pass through it, so when she is in a bad mood she wants to know what I do all day.

Just last month she give me a lot of her old clothes to send down for my children. So when she curse and quarrel I try not to let that bother me too much. I just swallow and bear it. When you is a forty-nine years old woman on a work permit, it different from being twenty-five or even thirty-five years old. When you is forty-nine years old, you have to be careful how you talk back to your employer. If they throw me out, tell me they don't want me to work for them anymore, then I don't know what I would do, because so many girls out there waiting to take my job that they wouldn't even miss me. For no one going to hire a fifty-year-old woman when women in their twenties are everywhere looking for work.

"She told me this is not the jungle"

So I am just trying to stick this out until I get my landed. I apply for my landed and I am doing a course in Health Care Aid. Something that will help me to get a job in a old people's home. I go to College two nights a week. So I am praying to the Lord that everything work out for me, that I pass the course and get my landed paper. I would still work in domestic work, because I don't have any education, and I don't know how to do anything else, or maybe I would work as a chambermaid in a hotel or continue domestic work, but as a day worker. I am never going to live-in again after I get those papers.

I want something where I can go home to my house at night. Close my door and pray to my God in peace. I want to know that when I go to bed at night, I don't have to listen out for people shouting at me to come and look after their food or to come and change diapers.

Right now my day begin at around 5:00 a.m. which is about when the baby wake up. He is seven months old. I share a room with him now, so when he wake up, I wake up too, and look after him, his cereal and feed him, usually he goes back to sleep until 7:30 a.m. or so. If he don't then I put him in his high chair and play with him. Sometimes I can put him back in his crib and he will just go back to sleep, but it all depends on his mood. Around 6:30 a.m. I prepare breakfast for the husband — eggs, coffee and toast — and then sometimes I make his lunch for him to carry.

Sometimes he will come home for lunch with his client. Then I make soup, a salad, depending on what he wants to eat. In the morning too, I usually dress the three boys, feed them and send them off to school. The school is close to home; in the winter I walk them back and forth, but in the spring and fall they go by themselves. During the summer they go away to camp for two weeks then I have them for the rest of the summer. Oh my God, they can really drive me crazy then.

Sometimes I just want to hit them, but I remember they is not my own, and their mother won't like it. Sometimes they is rude to you and you just want to discipline them, sometimes when they can't get their own way they will call me 'nig', I know they mean nigger but I pretend I don't hear. I remember once I complain to their mother and she told me that I was too picky that they are little boys and they would grow out of it, so now I don't bother to complain.

The wife gets up around 9:30 a.m. She owns a business. I make her breakfast, which change from one day to another, depending if she is still on her diet or not. She usually want fresh squeezed orange juice in the morning so I usually squeeze it for her. She leave for work about 10:00 a.m. When she leave I usually take a break, drink a little tea and look after my breakfast. Then the rest of my work start. I make up beds, wash dishes, clean the kitchen floor, vacuum the carpet, you name it. Twice a week I wash the clothes and iron them. Mostly the children clothes. Most of the missis and mister clothes I take to the dry cleaners.

One thing I don't like though, is that I have to wash her nylons and her panties and brassieres by hand. One day she ask me how I wash her panties and brassieres and I told her in the washer and she was very rude to me. I remember that night I went to bed and cry out to the Lord to take me out of that house. I remember she told me that her panties are not like my cloth ones and that this was not the jungle, but civilised North America, telling me that she only wear silk things which have to be hand washed. She also remind me of my age and told me she could get a younger person to take my job if I didn't want to wash her panties and brassieres by hand. These things I grin and bear. My only relief is when I get a chance to go to church on Sundays where I can cry out loud to the Lord and tell him my troubles. The church is my only peace, when I go on Sundays I meet other girls who in the same position like me.

You know we meet and we talk and I feel better. I want this life to end though. Sometimes I say if it wasn't for the church I would probably be in 999.[1]

"Sometimes I feel weak. Getting up all hours of the night to attend to him while his mother sleep."

Sometimes I wish that I even had a little privacy in my room. But I can't even call it my room, because ever since I come here I have been sharing it with whoever was the baby at the time. You know I'm on call twenty-four hours a day, like this baby now, sometimes I feel weak. Getting up all hours of the night to attend to him while his mother sleep. The way she was crazy over the baby, you would think she would breast-feed him herself. I don't say anything though — is not my place to tell her what to do.

I don't have no privacy at all, every evening she come from work, she ask me if I open the window in my room and spray the room, it's as if I smell or something. I don't like that at all for I am a clean woman. I grow up five children and all five of them healthy and strong and none of them ever catch any disease. But, you see, you can't answer back, so what to do — I just have to grin and bear the insults.

She keep asking me if when I get my landed if I am going to leave them. I tells her no, that I will work for her as long as she wants me to. Let her go on and think that, for as I get my landed and pick up another job I gone.

Only a mad woman would stay in a situation like this. You know how much a month I get? I shame to tell anyone, I don't even tell my friends for fear they laugh at me. I get $260.00 a month, she claim she take out money for my food and board. I don't question it though, because out of it I gets to send home a little something for my two little ones. I just play dumb, for I know that I am suppose to get around $500.00 a month by law, but I can't afford to cause any disturbance now. So I keep quiet.

I can't even play my little pocket radio in my room at night for she says it will disturb the baby. The only peace I get is in church and when they all gone to work.

"Even before I get to fourteen years old, I know that I wouldn't ever go on to high school or university"

I came here because I think life would be better, thinking I would get a break in life, but, sometimes things just seem like they worse, I want a rest, life have been rough on me ever since I can remember. I had my first child when I was fourteen years old. It wasn't because I was bad and like man. God see and know that wasn't the case. When I was thirteen I was already working in somebody house to help my mother put food on the table for my younger brothers and sisters. I use to work for this lady and her husband and their two little girls. I use to clean the house for the couple and wash their clothes. It was hard work, because there was no washing machine. I had to wash them by hand. One day the man force himself on me and got me pregnant. I didn't even know about child and man then. It just happen. After that the other four children came, right after one another, for I didn't know about birth control. You know, you keep going back to man after man, hoping that you'll get a little support and that things will be better for the children. But it don't work. I am glad I found the Lord and he help me to overcome those thoughts. My two youngest children live with one of my sisters. The other three on their own with families.

I tell you, when I see how my life has been wasted and I look and see the same things happen to my children and know that it going to happen to their children, I just get sad. Who is to blame? I never call this all on myself. I never wanted to have five children; but this is the life of poor people. We don't have anybody to push for us. Even before I get to fourteen years old, I know that I wouldn't ever go on to high school or university. When I was growing up, I remember mam and paps always worrying where the next pot of food would come to feed us all. There was no money around to school us properly.

When I get my landed, I want to save some money so that my grandchildren will be able to go to high school. This is my dream to see them graduated from high school ... maybe even get to go to university. I don't want them to do domestic work. Right now, I have four girls and one boy, and two of the girls working as day worker in St. Vincent. I don't want that to happen to my grandchildren. You know for me personally, it's not that I hate domestic work because that is the only thing I ever learn to do, but it's just the treatment that people dish out to you, you know they treat you worse than how they treats their dog or cat. If we could just be treated with a little respect, a lot of us would stay in domestic work.

I just hope that landed come through soon. You know sometimes I feel like a slave, sometimes I dream about freedom. You know, I wish I could move where I want to, work in whichever job I want, and have a little apartment on my own.

"Who but the Lord is going to listen to a fifty-year-old servant?"

Just the other day, I hear that the Immigration making it hard for women who are over forty-five and women with more than two children to get their landed. I don't know if it is true, but I hear a lot of girls talking about it. It really worry me, for I wonder if they already stamp my passport for me to go home, or if all this is rumour. They say that Immigration say any woman over forty-five soon can't clean house and will be just a burden on the government, and women with over two children will bring them into the country and take away the opportunities other Canadian children have.

I don't know what to believe. It not in my hands to decide what will happen. So I just pray to the Lord to decide what is right for me. Only he know the suffering I have been through. Nobody else would ever understand. Is he who I talk to, is he who I cry and pour my soul out to. Who else going to listen to a woman without education? Who else going to listen to a fifty-year-old servant? Tell me who? You know, when I get depress I just sing that old spiritual, "I have a friend in Jesus," then I feel good again.

When you ask me to talk to you about my life, I remember I first said no, because I was frighten that the people I work for might read the book and recognise me, and that Immigration might find out and deport me. But you know, that night when I was in bed, it was like a voice come to me and say, "do it, tell your story, you can trust this girl." So, the next morning, I think about it some more, then when the mister and missis gone to work, I called you. You know, I feel better just talking to you, and I just hope and pray that people will read what we have to say. For it's not an easy life being a domestic worker living in people's houses.

When I get my landed, I have a little savings in the bank, and I want to buy a little colour T.V., a record player to play my religious music, and a nice bedroom set. I'm tired of sleeping on a single bed. I'm going to rent a little bachelor apartment and really fix it up nice. Then I want to save the rest of my money to pay for my grandchildren's high school education.

Julie

First, let me say, I have not objections to go back home. I don't hate home I don't have those kinds of feelings ... it just that I feel that I'm going home with nothing accomplished ... that I have wasted a couple of years of my life.

Julie is a short, twenty-year-old Black woman, who came to this country from Antigua when she was eighteen years old to work as a domestic worker on an Employment Visa. She has a dark brown complexion and a mobile, angular face. She wears a short cropped afro and her dark brown eyes are ever hopeful as she speaks.

When we met at my house, where the first interview took place, Julie was dressed in a dark skirt and an off-white jersey. She was accompanied by a young woman, whom she introduced as her friend and 'church sis-ter'. She asked if her church sister could sit in on the interview. I agreed.

It is the spring of 1982 and Julie has agreed to talk about her experiences as a domestic worker on the employment visa and some of the problems she has encountered with the Immigration department. She feels there are hundreds of others in her situation who have been given a 'raw deal' by Immigration and Manpower. She says she wants the Canadian public to read about her and others like her and help to "better conditions for domestic workers."

Julie is extremely calm as she talks to me, and I can't help wondering to myself, if this is the same woman who is to be subjected to deportation the very next morning. Julie is, however, concerned about the use of her real name. "It's O.K. with me, but my family won't like it. They don't want any publicity, they are afraid the Immigration may give them problems." (I might add here that Julie's sister and the rest of the family are landed immigrants.) We agreed that we would use another name. After twenty minutes we decided on Julie.

Julie is resigned, calm and tired. Before I turn on the tape she tells me that she has to go back to her country tomorrow morning. On the surface she seems to be half-hopeful that she will be able to stay on in Canada, but her suitcase is packed, her ticket bought (her sister lent her the money) and the plane leaves at 10:00 a.m. the next morning. We exchange addresses and I promise to send her a copy of the book. Amid the seriousness and the tension which the deportation order has brought on, we joke about her new name and hope she'll remember it when she reads her story.

This was in April 1982. I did not hear from Julie the next morning and I assumed she had left on the plane to Antigua. I made a mental note to get in touch with her lawyer and the Immigrant Women's Job Placement

Centre, who I knew were trying every possible means to extend her time here.

It is June 1982 — I pick up a community newspaper and read the headline: ANTIGUAN GIRL REFUSES TO LEAVE. I go quickly through the story and I realise it is Julie. I make about half a dozen phone calls to find her whereabouts. No luck. A week later the phone rings. I answer it, and it is Julie. We talk for a long time, she fills me in on all that has happened since we talked in April, and I tell her how very happy I am that she went public.

She says it took a lot of courage and convincing her family that this was the only way to go. We hang up after what seems like hours and promise to get together soon.

This is Julie's story:

APRIL 1982

"I want to do it for other women like myself"

I don't know how to start. I really want to do it for other women like myself who are in this situation ... but where do I start? Should I start about my problems now with the Immigration, or should I start with how I came here on the work permit.

I'm from Antigua. I came here to work as a nanny for my brother-in-law's sister. That was in 1980. But it seems that ever since I came here, I've been getting bad breaks.

My first two jobs were not what I imagined they would be. It seems that it was just problems after problems, and now this problem with the Immigration.

If I had knowed that I would have all this problems, I would never come here. It's not as if I was starving in my country. I was employed as a typist. It's just that my dream all through my life, since I was a little girl, was to become a professional secretary. This was one of the reasons why I really left that job in Antigua because I felt up here I had opportunities.

It was always my dream to go to college and I knew that I could never have afforded it back home, and I really wanted so bad to be a professional secretary. Back in Antigua I come from a Christian home. I am the last of five kids. My father is a carpenter and my mother is a housewife. We were happy and lived comfortable, but there was just not enough money to send me to a secretarial school. Even before I left Antigua, I ask the person who I was coming up to, if I would be able to go to school.

Well, when I came to Canada, I stayed with the lady and her husband for about eight months, but she wasn't very nice and she told me to leave because I wasn't good enough for her kids.

When I went there in the beginning everything was fine, and they treated me O.K., but after a while I found out that I didn't have any real privacy and that really bothered me. One of the main things that happened why I had to leave was an incident involving my suitcase which someone in the house had broken into. The lady I worked with used to go into my suitcase and search my things.

Well, first of all, it was four of us in the house, me, the couple I was working with and a little baby who I was looking after. My boyfriend use to write me frequently and every time he wrote me, I would put my letters in the suitcase, then I would lock it because that was really the only privacy I had. One weekend I went to visit my sister and when I came back it was evident that someone had broken into my suitcase. I was really mad. I was burning because that was really the only privacy I had. Well, the wife wasn't home when I returned, so I went and asked the husband if someone had broken into the house or something. He said he didn't understand so I explained to him that I kept my things locked in my suitcase and my lock was broken off. He said nobody else in the house lost anything, and that the place wasn't broken into, and that it's strange that only my suitcase was broken into. He said that when his wife came home he would ask her about it. I was so upset that I went back out, and I didn't come back home until night, so I wasn't there when he asked his wife.

The next morning she just never talked to me. It went on like that for an entire week. I felt so alone and upset. That whole week I kept wondering if I did the right thing by saying anything about my suitcase being broken into. Well, about the second week she called me and said she understood that my suitcase was broken into. I said yes, and she said how it is quite funny and strange, and she wouldn't like to think that I broke into my own things and then try to say that it was her child who did it. I can't describe to you how I felt, I couldn't believe what I was hearing. This was impossible, because the baby was about one year old, and my suitcase had a lock on it, so it wouldn't be the baby. She said it wasn't her and on and on.

After that day, if I even pick up as much as a cup, I always pick up the wrong thing. Anything I did from that day on, it was wrong. Until one day she said to me I am not the person she wanted to look after her child.

I felt sad. I felt I was kind of alone in the world. I started to wonder what was it I really did wrong. I was wondering all over again if I shouldn't have said anything. I wondered if I should ask her to give me another chance. I guess it was best that I left, because after that incident, the communication broke down and we just never had anything to say to each other.

"I never had any privacy at all but I didn't want to make any trouble"

I went down to the Immigration and reported it. They gave me two weeks to find another job. Well, through some people at the church that I attend, I got a job with a family who had two children. When I started the people said they would pay me $82.00 a week. Well, I went there, and I started living-in and when I got my pay I noticed that I was only getting $50.00 a week. I stayed there for eight months and all through that eight months I was getting $50.00 a week. When I was working there, I looked after two kids. One was six years old and the other one year old.

I'd say my day started at about 7:30 in the morning when the kids got up and I would work until about 6:00 p.m. when my employers came home from work, but that depended from day to day, because sometimes they came home later. They just took it for granted that I didn't have anyplace to go, even though they never asked me if I had anywhere to go.

While I was there I had to share my room with the six-year-old boy. The little one-year-old girl had a bedroom by herself, but I had to share with the six-year-old son. They never told me this before they hired me. And they never told me why. The same day I went there to work they showed me the room and said that I had to share. I never had any kind of privacy at all, but I didn't want to make any trouble by asking why I had to share with the little boy, plus I didn't want to go back to Immigration again because I was afraid they would get fed up with me. But I didn't like it, it was not even as if it was my relative. We both slept on separate beds but I had no space to put my things because the drawers that were in the dresser had all the little boy's clothes.

I use to look after the kids everyday: feed them, and cook, and sometimes I cleaned the house. They never really actually came to me and say you have to clean, but you know, you would be in the house all day, and the house would be dirty so I just cleaned it up. Well after I left them, I heard through somebody at the church, that they said that I wasn't even cleaning the house everyday, that I was just looking after the kids but yet I wanted a raise. That was a lie. I know that I use to do a lot. I use to make up beds every morning. Everybody's beds, including the husband and wife. But to tell the truth, after a while I stopped doing it for the husband and wife because I realised that they were just using me. But I still made up the kids beds.

When I first went there I use to wash the dishes, vacuum the place, help with the laundry and cook the food. I'm not lying, I use to do everything. After a while, I just stopped because I realised that it was not appreciated, it was as if I was expected to do all this for $50.00 a week.

I use to get Friday evenings off and then I would go back to work Sunday night. I went to church every Sunday, mostly for recreation and the fact that I was a Christian from back home.

There was a lot more places that I wanted to go to, but I couldn't because I just didn't have any money. Fifty dollars a week just don't go far. Out of that $50, I had to send a little home to my mom because she had borrowed my air fare from the bank and she had to be paying them back, plus I was taking a dicta-secretarial course which I had to be paying for. So you know after all that I didn't have any left for recreation.

How I leave the job is that they passed the new law where you could apply for your landed status after you are here two years. I realised that my two years would soon be up. I also knew that when I applied for my landed they were going to tell me that I had to be working for a certain amount of dollar and that I would be in trouble because I wasn't getting minimum wage. That was when I went to my employer and asked them for a raise in my pay. I told them about Immigration and that I had to be working at minimum wages to apply for landed.

Well, I had no success. So I decided to start hunting for a job that would pay me the amount that Immigration wanted me to earn. So I left the job in February 1982, and I went into Immigration and told them that I wanted to apply for my landed after the two years were up, and that the Immigration policy say I have to be making about $500.00 a month in order to apply. So the officer said O.K. and gave me two weeks to find another job. The officer I that I saw at Immigration gave me a letter to give to Canada Manpower saying that if any jobs come up they should make them available to me.

When I took the letter to Manpower, the Manpower lady told me that they had two jobs available but I had to be a landed immigrant or a citizen to get them. I showed her the letter from Immigration, and told her what the Immigration officer had told me. She said the Immigration officers don't know what they are talking about. So then you know, I just left it at that. I figured that Immigration just pulling a trick on me.

So I went looking other places for jobs. I looked through the newspapers, I went to agencies, everywhere. Eventually I got so frustrated because I would call a few places, then they would say come for an interview, and after a while, after the interview, they would say that they would get in touch with me, and then when they do call they are not paying the money that the Immigration department require them to pay domestic workers on the work permit.

The Immigration department say they must pay $500.00 a month but a lot of them are paying $300.00 a month. For me alone, I would have been satisfied, because I wanted to stay here. Of all interviews I went on, which was about twenty, only two were paying the $500.00 a month, and I never heard from those two again after the interview, because they usually have a large selection of women to choose from.

They're in the minority, the people who is paying the $500 a month. So here I am without a job.

"So many jobs came close"

If I had heard about the centre, probably I would have been able to get a job a long time ago, because they would have helped me more than Manpower. But I didn't learn about them until the last few days when I was really desperate.

I also signed up with a lot of agencies that got jobs for nannies, but I didn't have any luck there either. I called them every day, but still I didn't get a job. Sometimes when I call up they would say that the job was gone, but yet I would see it in the papers days after. So I would call them up again and ask them how come I called up and they said the job was taken, and yet there is the ad in the paper. Then they would say it was not my type of job.

One day I asked the lady what they meant by not my type of job. Then she told me that those jobs that weren't my type don't give weekends off. So I said to her, "I'm not too particular about getting weekends off, as long as I got Sunday off." So then she said she didn't realise that. Well, I didn't hear from them again. I called up a lot more but it was always a different story. I went to another agency and they said they can't get in touch with the people who I gave her as references.

I then went back to Immigration to tell them that I couldn't find anything, and ask if they could help me. Somebody there asked me how come I didn't want to go back home. So I told them that when they passed the new law I felt that I could get to stay and I told them about my plans to go to school. I told them because of that I was willing to stay on in Canada and stick out any rough situation.

Well, my time was running out fast. I went back to the Immigration again, and I told them about the difficulty I was having in finding a job, and they told me I had a week to get out of the country. By this time I had been looking for a job from February to April and couldn't find any, because nobody was paying even the minimum wage.

I had so many jobs that came close but never really materialised. I remember this person was suppose to hire me and when I went into the Immigration to tell them they told me that I came in too late. You see, I didn't know that I had to be there at 7:00 a.m. or 8:00 a.m. if I wanted my papers processed the same day. So they told me to come another day. When I reached home I called the person who was going to employ me and told her what happened, she said that she didn't need me anymore, that she couldn't wait any longer.

I went back in to Immigration, I told them I was still looking and couldn't find anything because I had lost the job earlier in the week because they couldn't process my papers that same day when I came in. They didn't want to listen to what I was saying, they kept telling me that I had to get out of the country the next day or I would be deported. I told the Immigration officer that I didn't have money to buy a ticket or anything and he told me that that was not his business.

"I feel I have wasted a couple of years of my life"

I came home from the Immigration department feeling quite dull. I didn't have any money. Nothing. And I had nowhere to turn to. I just sat at home feeling really dull, not knowing what to do next, who to call. Then, for some reason, a long time ago I had taken down the phone number of a community agency that I didn't really use, so I said to myself I wonder if they would know anything like what to do. So I just called them out of curiosity. Well, the lady took my name and said she would call me back, and that even made me feel lower and sadder, because at that moment I felt that it was just one of those things again where they take your name and then they won't call you back. But the lady kept her word because she called me back the same night and she made arrangements for me to go and see a counsellor at a community agency and also to go see a lawyer.

So the next morning I got up early and the first thing I did was see the counsellor. She gave me the name of a lady who wanted a housekeeper. I left the office right away and went to see the lady who had the job. But when I went to see her, she said that she already got someone for the job, but when she hears my story she said that she would take me on because she really wanted to help me out. So I went to see the lawyer that same day too, and the lawyer and myself went to Immigration. Well, the Immigration officer said if I brought in the job offer, you know, the job letter from the lady he would cancel my deportation and put me back on the work permit.

We left the Immigration, and we tried to get the job offer and take it back to Manpower the same day, but it so happen that the woman who I was suppose to start working with lives in the suburbs and I couldn't get there in time to pick up the letter and back down before the office close. She called the office to tell them, but they said they were quite busy and they didn't have any other appointment to give us until a month later. Myself and the lawyer went back in and told the Manpower people that we would like the date moved up. The Manpower lady said that she could move the date up if Immigration called her. We left the Manpower office and went down to Immigration that same day. When we got to Immigration we got a new officer and he said that I had to get out of the country by midnight, and that there is no way that they could change me back from a visitor's permit, or from a deportation order to a work permit again.

I am telling you, that day seemed like the longest day in my life. I made so many trips to different places — from Manpower to Immigration — to this place and that.

After Immigration told me I had to get out, the lawyer called the Minister's office in Ottawa. She didn't get to speak to him so she spoke to some other person, and the person told her that since my passport had expired they would give me an extra two weeks in the country to get my passport ready, and then I had to leave the country. The lawyer said she would use the two weeks to try to appeal my case, that the Minister was giving the case to some other person.

The Immigration officer calls and bugs me every day to come and report to her, she wants to make sure I come out of the country.

So in the meantime, I borrowed some money from family here and I booked my flight. Right now, I am trying to cope with the fact that I am going home. First, let me say I have no objections to go back home. I don't hate home. I don't have those kinds of feelings. It's just that I feel that I'm going home with nothing accomplished, that I have wasted a couple years of my life, and I don't know when I go home what I am going to meet, what it's going to be like. It's like you have to start life all over again, or at least a part of your life all over again and that can really hurt and be painful, especially if you had planned a certain part of your life.

"Now all my dreams — just crushed"

I really wanted to finish school. If I had felt that I couldn't, I would not have bothered to come. Sure it was fine to stay in the house all day looking after babies, but I didn't want to do that for years and years, especially after I realised that there were absolutely no guarantee that I would get my landed. I really decided from back home, that if I got the chance to come up I would go to school so that when it was time for me to go back home, at least I had something to show.

So when I got the opportunity to come up here, I said to myself, well I am on a good ground and everything. I'm going to get life started. And when I am finish college, I felt that probably I might get on to go to university, especially when I heard about this new policy. I said to myself I like travelling and eventually I would get to travel. Now all my dreams — just crushed. I feel bad, really bad. If I had finished school I could say that it's not too bad because at least I could say I have achieved something since I've been here.

When you go home the first thing they are going to ask is where were you working. And you don't even have a piece of paper to show that, even though you worked as a nanny, you were going to school and upgrading your skills.

That's why I was so happy when I eventually saved up enough money to enroll in a college. I have already invested $700.00 in the course. I was taking dicta-secretary. I started the course last year and if I continue I would be finished by the middle of this year. The course has eaten up all my money. All along I was trying to get something worthwhile in my head, that even if I had to go back home eventually then I would have had something to go home to. But now, I don't know. Well, I have a little office skill because I worked as a typist before I came here, so I know I have that little skill, but I still wanted something else you know and that was why I started to take this course at college. Now I'll have to leave all of that and go home with nothing.

I have nothing to show. Absolutely nothing. I'll just have to go home and depend on pull string to get jobs which I hope might be successful.

I thought of going into the college and talking to them, but I don't know how much they could do, because those Immigration officers are real creeps and they don't care. So I don't know. If I go home, maybe, I'll get a chance to come back up and finish my diploma.

POSTSCRIPT

Julie is now back in Antigua. Her appeal to the Immigration department to renew her permit fell on deaf ears. She was told by Immigration officials that she could voluntarily go back to Antigua or be deported. She was informed that upon deportation she could never apply for admission to Canada. She chose the former option, hoping desperately that she can someday re-apply as a foreign domestic worker on the employment visa.

Angel

> My employer is nice and she's understanding ... she is very encouraging. She did encourage me to get my licence. So now I can drive.
> She said to me, "Learn to drive, because it's nice when you can master your own self, it makes you less dependent."

Angel is a warm, friendly, thirty-one year old Black woman who talks easily and spontaneously. She is slim, about 5'3" tall, and wears her short cropped hair in an afro. Angel works as a live-in domestic for a family of four in the north-east section of the city.

We first met at the Jamaican Canadian Association's domestic workers' meeting, an initiative of Eva Smith, a former domestic worker herself, and at the time an employee of the JCA. I was first attracted to Angel by her warm and open smile. After the meeting she found her way over to me before I had a chance to call her. She introduced herself and expressed her excitement and her willingness to talk about her life as a domestic worker on a work permit: "You won't believe this, but this is something I always say I want to do. I've always wanted to write my life story, but I just didn't know how to go about it."

We arranged to meet and talk. Angel suggests my house. Before we part, I thank her many times for her openness and her enthusiasm.

It is the winter of 1982. The day we schedule our meeting turns out to be very cold, and I wonder if Angel will show up. It's Sunday, our appointment is for eleven in the morning, and I see no sign of her. I understand because the weather is bad. I promise myself that I will call her Monday morning to make another appointment.

It's eleven-thirty and there is a knock at my door. I pull the curtains aside and there is Angel, shivering, but still holding on to that million dollar smile.

Angel has been in Canada almost five years, working as a domestic on a Temporary Employment Visa. She is still employed by the same family. As the tape spins, Angel talks about her boyfriend and children back home, the loneliness that comes about after being separated for so long from her children, the youngest of whom is six years old. She talks about her parents and the obstacles her mother confronted as a single mother and as a domestic worker, about her father and his relationships with women. She is candid and unabashed about what it's like growing up in the Caribbean and her struggle to guide the course of her life, her struggle to make it different from that of her mother. Finally, Angel talks about her work here as a domestic, her relationships with her employers and their children, and her hopes for the future and bringing her family closer to her in Canada.

CHILDHOOD

"My father didn't get along with no woman"

I was born in Kingston, Jamaica on February 3, 1950. I have twelve brothers and sisters on my mother's side and seven brothers and sisters on my father's side. I was grown up with a father, not a mother. I was happy with some part of my childhood, but I was unhappy with a lot of things too. Still, I am thankful for my father. Presently, he's at home in Jamaica, he's blind, and I am taking care of him.

Even before I came to Canada he was living at my house with my children and my boyfriend.

We had hard times, me and him. Every time I go back home we still have that hard time because he is domineering, he loves to have his own way. On his side I am the fourth in line, and on my mother's side, well, I don't even know because my father and mother didn't really get along.

He didn't get along with no woman. He was a very wild man and that was one of the reasons why he and all his girlfriends eventually broke up. He was wild and he always wanted to tell them what to do. He had a lot of girlfriends, and he wanted them all to be content with him. He was also married and a lot of his women didn't know he was married. His wife and kids lived in the country and he worked in town. My mother didn't even know he was married until she started having us. He didn't tell her a thing. (Now he is separated from his wife, but they are not divorced.) My father and mother lived together when she was pregnant, but when my brother was three months old she had to walk out on him. I was one year old. She never came back to live with us. I never really knew her, but I grew up knowing of her because she use to visit us. All in all, she had twelve children.

When she walked out and left me and my brother, she also left us with one other child, my father's child that he had taken from her mother. It was we four who grew up together.

When I was a little girl, I use to feel angry with her for leaving us, but as I got older, I learned to appreciate her. Like I said, she had twelve children. Right now she lives alone. Some of the children grew up with her, but she had to leave some in the country with their fathers so she could go to the city to find work. She use to work looking after her brother's children because their mother had died.

Life was a bit ugly for my mother, especially when you hear her talk of her experience. My father said she deserted her children to go look after her brother's children, but that wasn't it. She had to make a living, and she couldn't do domestic work and carry all her children along with her. Life was really ugly for her, that's all I can say. It's like you go for help, and then you end up with a help-weight — getting more babies. I think that was one of the problems. I have forgiven her for everything, because it wasn't really her fault. Men back home beat women really bad, and he did her all those kinds of things — and not only she, but almost all of his other girlfriends.

Once I heard him tell my brothers that when he was their age he had a lot of stripes.[1] And then my mother use to give me terrible stories about him. She told me that he use to be with all the single women in the tenement yard.[2] But to be honest, I've grown to love him. I love him very much. I love my mother, but there is something special that I feel for my father. Don't care how much he hurts me, I could never turn my back on him.

"My ambition was to be a fashion designer"

When I was growing up, my ambition was to be a fashion designer. I loved it so much. I remember when I left primary school, I had to sew my uniform to go to high school. It was my dressmaker who taught me part of the sewing. I use to go and visit her often, and she use to give me paper to cut my high school uniform on. Sometimes it was too big because I didn't know about measurements, so I use to just cut it how I knew to cut a blouse, and then she would shape it for me. Then I remember sewing dresses for myself and shirts for my brother. Now I can't even cut anything. I say to myself that I should have kept it up, but you get so despondent when you see a lot of things doesn't get to go your way. Having children was probably one of the reasons. You have them so fast. When I got pregnant with my first child I wasn't ready. I told the baby's father this, but he said he was ready because he thought he was big enough to have children.

My father was one of the faults. I really wanted to continue my education. I wanted to go to commercial school. My father said, "Stay home and do the housework." I'll never forget those words. He thinks he didn't say it, but it was me who heard it.

I only spent two years at high school. Then I got a job at a restaurant for my summer holidays. At that time you could get holiday jobs easy. After that job I never worked in Jamaica again.

"I wanted somebody who was up there"

It was around this time that I met my boyfriend. I was fifteen years old. He's really from the country, but he grew up in Kingston, and we were living close to each other. I'm from between the ghetto area and the good area. I met him on the road. I use to go to Girl Guides meeting, and I met him one night as I was coming home. That night I was in a bad mood, so he called to me, and I said something bad to him. I wasn't even thinking about what I said. Still, every Monday night he would set out for me coming from Guides' meeting. I didn't want to talk to him because I remember my father saying, "Don't talk to any of the boys on the road." But eventually we started to talk, he finally got to me. We started writing letter to each other and my girlfriend would take them back and forth for us because I couldn't let my dad know what I was doing. He didn't like the guys who hung out on the road.

I had another boyfriend before I started talking to this one. My aim in life was that since I didn't have a lot of education and because life was so poor for me, I wanted somebody who was up there. The first boyfriend I had was really qualified. He went to St. Andrew Technical School. At the time the Jamaica School Certificate had just come out and he got ten passes. He was in the news media all over. I really like him, and I would always say to myself, "He's gonna be my husband." When he ask me to be his girlfriend I was glad. He wanted to be an engineer and he said he wanted to come to Canada. He ended up teaching in Jamaica instead.

When he entered college to become a principal, he became so much of a big man that he started having a lot of girls and then I didn't see him often. That was when I started talking to this other guy. But I always remember praying at nights, asking the Lord to choose for me, to decide which one should be my husband.

"I didn't want to have a split family"

I was brought up in a Christian background and every night we had to pray as a family. When I was growing up, I was brought up to think it was sex after marriage, so I use to say, "Lord, whoever I have my children for, let that man be my husband." I didn't want to have a split family, I didn't want to have children for one man and then children for another man. I didn't like the way I was grown up and I wanted my children to grow up differently.

I eventually got pregnant for my second boyfriend. I really love him because he was so patient. When he proposed sex to me, I told him I was a Christian. I use to give him books to read about how a boy meets a woman and then he never really ask me for sex again. Eventually a year pass before he really ask again, and then he didn't even ask, because we were in such a spot that there was no other choice.

I got pregnant. I was seventeen years old then. My father reacted very funny toward my boyfriend. He didn't like the boy because he said he was always on the road. He still doesn't like him.

I love my boyfriend very much, but we had some really rough times together. During the time that I was pregnant for him, he had another girlfriend who was also pregnant. Our babies were born five months apart. It was awful, it was embarrassing, and the girl lived close to me too. Sometimes I could see her when she passed by my house.

Every time I made up my mind to leave him he would tell me that it was me who he loved. There was a lot of things that was bothering me over the ages, he was a wild guy, and by then he had two other children outside. I couldn't understand him. In the end it seemed like I always forgive him so I ended up having four kids for him. My youngest child was born in 1976 and to be honest, by then I was very frustrated. I was tired of sitting down every day not doing nothing. I wanted to make myself a woman. At that time all the birth control that I could use was against my health. When I went to the family planning clinic, they gave me condoms, and you know it's not every man wants to use that. So then I use to use this birth control called bat and draw,[3] but it didn't work. Then when I came to Canada I got to understand that the birth control pill they had in Jamaica at the clinic is not the same kind you get here. Back home I heard that the pills were not good for me because they had something in them that affects the heart. Then there was the injections.[4] That was definitely out, I would never take them. And he would never use the condom. They only had the pill, the injections and the condom in Jamaica, so we used our own method which was bat and draw. It worked for about three years, but then it never worked again.

When I was pregnant this last time in 1976, I always say to the Lord, "Lord, I wish it is a boy," because then I could go out and do anything. I could leave him at a younger age. I was tired of staying home. I was so happy when I found out he was a boy.

Shortly after that I started working for a friend. She had a business, just a small factory, they mill corn for animals. Her business was small so she started me off at $15.00 a week, when business picked up and when minimum wage went to $24.00 she gave me that. My boyfriend didn't know how much I was working for, I couldn't tell him or he would be mad. I wanted to get away so bad that I didn't mind working for that. The work was hard. I had to sew bags and the place was dusty and I had corns on the palm of my hand. It was those big power machine that I had to use, but you get use to it, it's your job. I got to enjoy it. I use to help the guys with the corn after I sew the bags.

There were guys there who use to cheat her, there were some nice ones too. Sometimes I would sit with them and talk about the Bible because I was an Adventist at that time. We grew up as a religious family, but it was a girlfriend that introduced me to the Adventist faith. She asked me to come with her one night. I went and for me the message was good and I also proved it.

I spent about a year working with my friend. It was a lucky thing that I was saving my wages because we had to move. The government was on this clean-up programme and where we were living was one of the areas that had some very bad houses. I took my wages and I fix the bed, the chairs and the tables and they were in good condition. I was glad that I had saved up that money or we couldn't have them fixed. When we moved they looked like new furniture.

It was really after we moved from our old neighborhood that the kids' father and I started living together. My father didn't really like him, and even when I was pregnant I lived at home.

"I was glad when she said she would sponsor me"

My sister wrote me one day in 1978 and told me that she wanted to give me a treat to show how much she appreciated me taking care of her kids. She said she would send me a ticket to come to Canada on a holiday. I didn't want to leave Jamaica and I kept saying, "If I am not coming to Canada legally, then I don't want to travel at all." She said for me to come on a holiday to see if I like it.

Finally, I came on a holiday for seven weeks in 1978. When I came I found that I really liked it, it was nice and clean. My sister found me a job, with a lady, and I worked with her for about five weeks, but I was scared that Immigration would find out that I was working without a permit. So I told the lady I was going to go home. She asked me if I wanted to come back to work for her and I told her yes. She said she'd look about sponsoring me on the work permit.

To be honest, I was glad when she said she would sponsor me because I wanted to get away from my boyfriend. Not that I hated him. I love him, but I didn't want to get pregnant again, and when I wanted to get married, he didn't want to marry, then when he wanted to get married, I didn't, so I got so frustrated. The poverty life was really getting to me, we were getting older and the kids were getting older. I wanted a better life for them. Coming to Canada on the vacation and seeing how the life can be so decent — when I look back home how people living and we can't reach anywhere, I just wanted to leave. And then he was such a gambler. He always gave me house money and anything I need for the kids, but my house wasn't really what I wanted it to be. It was all of those things that made me decide to come to Canada.

When my papers finally come through my boyfriend's mother promised to come to the house and help out with the kids. She goes home to her house on weekends. This was really helpful of her because my boyfriend is a jeweller and he comes home late in the evening. If his mother wasn't there, there would be nobody to take care of the kids.

For the first year I was depressed a lot of times. I started to save my money and when I got my holidays I went home. I just felt like I didn't want to stay in Canada any longer. My family really missed me, they needed me so much — especially my two oldest daughters because they were going through the stage where they really need parents to guide them and their father doesn't really understand them that much. He is responsible, but he is not stern and he needs someone to motivate him. He doesn't really understand them because they all just started living together a few years back. Before I had all the kids, I use to say to him, come and let us live together. He wasn't listening then and by the time he really wanted to, I was scared because by then I had the kids and I was pregnant. When you go out looking a place, the owners don't want women with children and stomach in their homes. He use to say I was coward, but I knew what I was talking about. When he did step in, it was a bit too late. But, thank God, I don't think it's that late because the children understand a bit now.

"The only problem is my day off"

My employer and her husband have three kids — thirteen, ten and seven years old. I do the whole housekeeping — I clean, cook, wash and look after the children. I don't cook for she and her husband, only for the kids and myself and tidy up everything. We have a cleaning lady who comes in once a week to do the general cleaning. I try to be very reasonable. Sometimes I haven't got anything to do and then I'll do something like the windows. I don't go way up, I do what is in my hand reach, and if I have spare time left over, I'll clean out the cobwebs in the ceiling, I won't wait until the cleaning lady comes. I do these extra little things because my employer isn't the type that will come in and wipe her fingers around the edge of a piece of furniture to see if I dusted it. Sometimes I go a little overboard because, like I said, she is reasonable, but I'm living in the house and I want the house to look lookable so that people can come in and know she have a clean house.

The only problem, really, is my days off. I get half days on Friday, Saturday, and Sunday. When I take my half day on Friday, what I do is to go and do a part-time job. If I didn't then I would have the whole afternoon not doing anything on Friday.

My employer's nice and she's understanding. If I'm having problems with home and she sees that I am a bit upset or if it seems like I heard bad news, she'll ask me how are the kids back home, she'll find out if everything is O.K. She knew that my eldest daughter was giving me a hard time. She'll talk to me and she'll encourage me. That really helps because kids get to you sometimes.

She makes her kids have respect for me. The first time I started working there, I was vacuuming one day — she was home then, she wasn't working and her daughter came in and was screaming. I don't know what she was saying, whether she was saying something dirty about me or what — but her mom came out and I saw her mom grab her and took her upstairs. I turn off the vacuum and her mother said, "Apologize to Angel, tell her you are sorry." And she apologized. I didn't ask what it was because I didn't hear it. After that the kids didn't show me any signs of prejudice for being Black. I know that in the beginning the kids feel some kind of prejudice because they learn it at school. I don't want to blame them, but I remember how it was when I came first.

Now it is different, but when I just came here, the kids' friends would come home and they would say something funny — I didn't hear it, but I could feel it. Now the older girl never really come out and say anything about my colour — she's older and she understand why I'm Black — but the little boy will ask me. One day he ask me, "Why are you Black, Angel and I am white?" I ask him the same question and he doesn't know, so I say, "Listen, God didn't make all of us the same colour. You get your complexion because of the different climate you live in. My people weren't from Jamaica, they were from Africa. They are dark — some have straight hair and some have curly hair — but they are all dark because of the climate. Sometimes you will see very fair skinned or whites down there, but that's because of a lot of mixing with different nations." He says, "I can't see how come you're Black and I am white." I say, "We all have one God and skin doesn't make any difference. When you cut your skin, what comes?" "Blood," he says. "The same thing that comes out when I cut mine. I've got everything like you, it's only the skin that's different." I guess now he understands, because he doesn't question me anymore. This friend of mine use to tell me that the little girl she look after use to say, "Maybe they went in the oven and baked and get Black."

But apart from what I've said, there has really been no prejudice in the house. Once I braided my hair, and this man came over to my employer's house to have dinner with them, and said, "Oh boy, isn't this girl pretty, she has a beautiful smile." And my employer said, "Oh, you want to hear her name. She's Angel." He said, "Oh my goodness." And my employer laughed and said, "You see ugly people around this house?"

Her husband is an engineer. I remember last summer they took me to Florida and it was very nice. When I came back, I thought that since they give me the trip, I wouldn't take my two weeks. But then when we came back she gave me my two weeks vacation and I said to her, "Don't bother." But she said, "Oh no, that's not fair because you were still working."

When I started working with her, on the paper it was $60.00 she was suppose to give me, but before I left Jamaica the woman at the Immigration say it was now $70.00 a week. So when I came up I say my wages is now $70.00 per week and not $60.00 and then she say O.K. Well, my OHIP, she pays part of it and then she pays half of my government taxes. Then in my next year there was another increase. That's the other thing, she never knows when I am to get an increase. So one day I was there and I say to her, "You know, it's time for me to get an increase," and she said, "O.K. I will talk to my husband and I'll get back to you." She was so nice, after that she gave me $95.00. Then she got a full-time job, I wasn't suppose to cook for the kids but I did it anyway — so she gave me an increase of $5.00 because I had to cook for the kids. Like I said, she's really nice. I can't stop saying it.

The only other thing is that sometimes she don't really know how to handle money, you know, like deductions and things like that. Like my taxes wasn't taken out because she hadn't got to clarify it as yet. So I'll have to pay back all of that five months money that I wasn't paying. But you know, in paying back that money, she doesn't take it all at once. She'll ask me how I want her to take it, because it was her fault. I remember one of the times she gave me an increase and I keep saying to her go find out how much tax you are suppose to take. But she didn't go, and then sometime later she found out she was taking less tax. Then she said to me, "O.K. Angel, you don't pay, it's my fault." And she paid it all. But you know, the good things she does and the way the family treats me with respect compensates for some of the other things, like the taxes.

I'm not really stern on my hours because I have my time in the day where I take my rest. Sometimes I'll be in the kitchen until 7:30 p.m. But I'm in there so late because when she comes in and she make supper for her and her husband, I clean up after. I'm not that exact that I'm just going to come in and wash up what I use and get out. I'll clean up what she uses, after I finish with that, I go and watch T.V. or I go to my room. Sometimes, if my T.V. isn't working on a station I will stay in the den and watch T.V. like I said. I am not under any stress, where I have to be working like a horse, and can't relax.

"I just pour myself out to God"

She is very encouraging. She did encourage me to go and do my driving lessons and get my licence. So now I can drive. She said to me, "Learn to drive, because it's nice when you can master your own self, it makes you less ... how do you say it ... less ... yes, less 'dependent'. Now I am going to school and I am doing this Women on Wheels course, because I figure if I am driving it's nice to know something about the car. Another thing, I must be honest with you. I don't mind living in, especially when it's cold. I rather stay in because the only days I go out is to put out the garbage and really if I wasn't going to school many days I would just stay in.

What I like about living in, and about this house too is that I am secluded to myself. My room is far from theirs. Like where we were living before, we were all on the same bedroom level, but now that we moved at this new house, my bedroom is to one corner and I have another entrance to take me out if I want. Many days she'll call me and tell me I can get a Wednesday off or take two evenings off, and then most time I just stay in my room, read because I like to read, or write letters and listen to the radio sometimes. I like doing that, because I find it very quiet and I can talk to God, and many days I just pour out myself to him.

When it's really cold outside, I don't mind going from work to church and then back home. But when it's nice out, I love to visit a lot of places that I don't know. I meet a few girlfriends that I met here in Canada, and we go out. Two of my girlfriends, I know from back home. They are all in the same domestic field. I also met one of my teachers from back home. I talk to her sometimes on the phone. She is working with revenue tax. I also met a lot of other small islands girls. I call them and keep in touch with them on the phone. You know, I love going to new places and meeting new people.

"We have to make sacrifices"

Since I've been here, I've met a lot of women in the same domestic work who have children back home like me. I joined the Domestic Workers' Group and through them I meet a lot of new people and get to understand their problems. I've learned a lot from those meetings. I didn't even know that I could be claiming for the money I send home to my kids on my income tax. If I don't come to the meetings, then I would be listening to the news media and getting my information from them and not even really understanding it.

You know, every time I go to the meeting and listen to other domestic workers, I say, "Thank God, mine isn't that bad," the only problem I have is just my days off, but apart from that I am very happy for the person I work with, because some of the women who come to the meeting have it hard. I've even heard stories of women who have to sleep in the same room as the dog, and you know, a lot of them are scared to talk about this to Immigration because they don't want to be deported, because their family are depending on them to send money home for them live on.

I don't really feel lonely anymore. But the first two years, I was really lonely. I was so depressed. It still really breaks my heart though, when I hear my boyfriend's voice on the phone. It hurts so much to leave the kids. When

I went back home in '81 for Christmas, they were crying and telling me, "Don't go back to Canada. Take us with you. We want to be with you. Can't you stay with us?" I said, "No, I have to go back. I know you're sad and so am I, but some day you'll understand." Saying that to them, especially the younger ones, really tore my heart, because I know that they didn't really understand. But you know, now I am stronger, and I keep saying to my boyfriend, "Listen, we have to make sacrifices. I want something for them, I want them to come here and then when they come here whatever they want they can choose, and then I will know that I did my part."

Savitri

I don't understand the Immigration, I don't know why they want to keep me away from my children and husband ... I want to know if when people read this book they can help to do something about this matter.

Savitri has not seen her husband and four children since 1979. She came here to work as a domestic worker on the Employment Visa, with the hopes of getting enough money together to help support her family and to eventually buy land to build a house for her family in Guyana. To be still here in 1983 was not a part of the plan. She thought she would have been able to make enough money to return to Guyana sooner. "When I just started with these people I got paid minimum wage, which use to work out to $510.00 or so a month, but I don't know what happen but for the last six months I've been getting $400.00 a month. I don't ask questions, because I don't want any trouble."

Savitri is in her late forties and is of East Indian descent. She is a plump woman who stands 5'3" tall. She wears her shoulder length hair which is showing signs of greying in a tight bun.

Savitri talks easily about her life, although at times, she seems nervous and anxious about her ability to express her feelings clearly. Her life seems complex, attending to her children's and husband's needs long distance — keeping the communication going between them — being mother, cook, and wash-maid to a Canadian family here, and struggling with the Immigration Department to review her files.

Her major problem at the moment is with Canada Employment (Manpower) and Immigration. She is worried that they might not give her landed status. She applied for landed status under the Domestic Workers' Program in February 1982 and has been having problems ever since. She feels that they are not too eager to process her papers for landed status because of her 'large' family and the possibility of them eventually immigrating to Canada. She is angry and upset. "I don't understand the Immigration, I don't know why they want to keep me away from my children and husband."

Here is Savitri's story:

LIFE IN GUYANA

"Things were hard for us as a family"

I been in this country about five years now, working on the work permit as a domestic. I came here because life at home was rough and it was easier for me to come up here and work than for my husband. I have a husband back in Guyana and four children. I have not seen them since I came up here in 1979. We write to each other and two times a year we talk on the phone.

Things were hard for us there as a family — my husband have a job back home, but sometimes when I was there things were slow, and he wouldn't have a job. He is a carpenter. So when I got the opportunity to come here on the work permit as a domestic, we all decided that it was the best thing for me to do. At least that way one of us would have a steady job and steady money coming in. I didn't expect to be here so long, though. I thought that I would be back home by now with my family, or else they would be up here with me, but as you see things didn't work out that way.

We try to write each other often, so we don't lose touch, and so I know what is going on with the children. My mother lives at the house with my husband, so that she can give a hand with the children to see that they don't lose their manners. I am glad I got the chance to come here because so far I have been able to send money home to my husband, even though it's not as much as I thought it would be, but it still helps to send the children to school. I miss them very much. This life is hard, really hard.

"They will call you to get them a glass of water"

Since I have been here I have work for only two different people. The work is hard, and with both of the family I work with, there was always problems when it comes to my days off. You know, just because you live in the house, they make you work like a horse all the time. Once you stay in that house on your days off, you know it's trouble you calling down on yourself because they always going to call you to come and do something for them. Little things that they could do for themselves, they will call you to do, like getting a glass of water for them, when the kitchen so close to the living room. But once they in front of the T.V. they don't want to leave it. It is really harassing, getting up and doing these things for them when I already work all day, but I just keep quiet. Right now I don't even get my full days off. I am entitled to two full days off, but instead, my employer told me that I must take two half days off. I don't say anything though, I just pretend that everything is fine. Because of that I don't get out much, except when I take the children to the park, and when I go to church. Once a week I buy toilet paper and soap and a T.V. guide for my room. And when the children want clothes, I go to Honest Ed and shop. I send home a parcel for them two times a year, in July and in December. So you know, getting my full days off is not even my real problem. I get use to that in the five years that I been here. So I don't let it trouble me too much as long as I get to send money home to help my family. My husband trying to pay down on a piece of land to build a house, so that is why I keep quiet, because I don't want to move around too much, I don't want to create any bad feeling with the Immigration officers.

"People who read this book can help"

Now my real problem is getting my landed and is this I want to talk about because I want to know if when people read this book they can help to do something about this matter.

I go into Immigration since February 1982, to find out about this landed immigrancy business. They ask me to fill out a application and I fill it out, and I put down my husband and four children on the form. They ask me if my family would be eventually coming up and I tell them yes. They said they would get in touch with me, but after waiting months and months I didn't hear anything from them.

I went back down again in the month of July, and told them that I was taking a dressmaking course for my upgrading and that I had finished taking a St. John's Ambulance health care course. They write all that down in the files and said they would get in touch with me. Well, even in November 1982 I still didn't hear anything from them at all. So it was then that somebody from the Domestic Workers' Group gave me the name of a lady at a legal aid clinic to see. I went down and saw the lady and she took all the information and said she would write the Immigration for me, and find out what was wrong. She heard back from them fast, for it was the middle of November that I get a phone call from her to come in to see her. When I went she said Immigration had no record of my application. That's what they say. I don't know what happened to it because I know that I went in to see them and they write it all up, all the information that I give them. The lady at the legal aid office was very nice to me, and she and another Black lady, I think she is a community worker, went down to Immigration with me and they give me another form to fill out. It was just like the first form that I did fill out, so I fill it out again and hand it back to the officer. Then they call me January 1983 and said that they look over my files and that I must come for an interview. I went in alone for the interview. That was the longest interview I ever had in my life.

"Immigration officer say we don't know how to take good advice"

The Immigration officer had me in his office for three hours asking me the same question over and over again. Mostly he ask me about my husband and my children. He wanted to know first if I was going to bring up my family. I tell him yes, that I had put that down on the form. Then he ask me when was the last time I saw my husband. I tell him since I come up in 1979 I didn't see my husband, but that we write and talk on the phone. Then he ask me if I think my husband didn't have a girl back home. You know he just keep asking question like those. I was getting vexer by the minute. But I tried to keep cool, and answer him nice. He wanted to know if my children or my husband ever get in trouble with the law. I tell him no. Then he ask me why I didn't stay here and work in domestic work and try to save enough and then go home. He said it would cost me less if I did it that way instead of sending for the whole family to come up. Then he tell me he was just giving me a little advice and don't usually give out that kind of advice but is because he think I am an "intelligent girl." I just sit there dumb. Then he tell me to go home and think about it until they call me in again.

They call me again in April 1983 and that time I see a different officer, who ask me the same thing about my husband. I say they was coming up, and he get rude, and say we people don't know how to take good advice and that is why we suffer so much. I didn't know what he was talking about and then I remember my meeting with the first officer, so maybe they got together and talk. He told me if I was going to be so stubborn and not take good advice that it was my business, but that before they decide on my landed and my family that I have to get a job offer for my husband before he come into the country. So I leave the Immigration.

When I went home I told my employer about what the Immigration had said. I ask her if she could ask her husband if he could write a letter for my husband. Her husband run a cleaning company. You know, the ones that clean office and other work place in the night. For weeks I wait for an answer and didn't get any from her. So one night I approach her and ask her if she tell her husband. She pretend she had forgotten and said she would ask him right now. But I don't know, something was funny, and I just get the feeling that she did talk to him about it before. Both of them come in the kitchen where I was, and he said that he didn't need anybody else in his business and that if Immigration find out he was doing something like that they could get him in a lot of trouble.

He just kept talking like that for a long time, then he said he would do it because he really like me and the work I do. Then he said that he was going out of his way to do it, so I should also try to help him out too. Then both he and his wife stare at me. I ask him how he mean and he look at his wife. She said to me that he mean that I could help him clean two nights a week. I couldn't say a word. It just numb me, for I work like a real race horse in that house and I didn't know that they would ask me to clean office at night on top of that, but I really wanted that letter for the Immigration so that my husband could come up, so I tell them yes I would do it. The husband said for me to come down to his office the next morning and his secretary would type the letter for me. I go down and got the letter and take it straight over to Immigration.

"From I have been here I always work for my own bread"

I didn't hear anything from them after that, so I called them and they said that when they were ready to see me they would send a letter to me.

Well, three weeks ago I got a letter from them to come in. They say they checked out the letter and that it was O.K. but that now the problem was the children. They say they couldn't give the children landed, because they were big children. You know, that they were teenagers and that they were wondering what the children would do when they get here. The Immigration officer said again that his advice would be to let them stay in Guyana because the unemployment here was too high and they would come here and get frustrated and turn bad. He said I must take good advice and let them stay there with a relative and that my paper for me and my husband could come through quicker that way.

I couldn't sit still and listen to that, you know, because I come here five years ago and work my hands dry scrubbing other people floor and looking after their children, I didn't come here and thief or murder anybody so I didn't like the way he was talking to me, like I come here and beg the government to look after me.

From I have been here, I never sick one day, I always at work, working for my own bread. I couldn't sit quiet so I tell him that I want my children here with me, just like how he and his wife have their family with them, I tell him that we is not wild animal and that we know family life, too. Then I tell him good day and walk out of him office. So I don't hear anything since that, and is that I worried about now, for I don't know if they will hold all of that against me now.

But you know this time I couldn't sit quiet. I was trembling when I come out of the office. I even did expect a police or somebody to pick me up off the street and arrest me. All when I got home, I listen every time the doorbell ring to see Immigration officers coming for me to deport me. You know, they handle you like you is a piece of furniture. No respect at all.

But this thing really have me worried and I wonder if anyone, like people with a say, who the Immigration will listen to, can help me. I don't understand the Immigration, I don't know why they want to keep me away from my children and husband. They just feel that we are going to be a burden to the government, which is not true. Look how long I work in this country. Away from my family all this while and still they want me to stay away from them.

"Why are they doing this to me and my family?"

Right now I am very worried and troubled. For I feel that I might not get through with my landed, because Immigration don't want my children here.

I want my children to be able to come up here and get some of the opportunities like other children, especially in the schools. My younger daughter just graduated from high school and I am proud of her. I would very much like her to come up here and be able to get some of the opportunity to go on further in her education.

My youngest daughter is very bright too, she get high marks in school. I would like her to be able to come here to go on further. I don't want her brightness to go to waste; you know, so many children bright and because they don't get the education opportunity, they just don't bother to go to school and they get disinterested in life and end up sad and bitter. I see it happen too many times. I don't want that to happen to my children. I want to be able to be proud of them.

I feel that I have done my duty here and my children should get the opportunity to come here. I never get in any trouble here, and I always treat people with respect, so why are they doing this to me and my family? I never break one law in this country yet. I am so nervous. I can't breathe sometimes when I think that my children might not get through to come. I feel like a piece of meat that is squeezed between two pieces of bread.

"I don't want to die in this country"

After my papers come through, I want to stay here and work until I am about sixty-four years old and then I want to go back home. I don't want to die in this country, or be a old person in this country, things too lonely for old people here, it's not like back home where you have a lot of people to talk to; here they put you away in old people's home. I want to go back home to grow old and die. The dirt too cold here to be buried in. That is why I say that when I get my landed, I am going to rent a room — a furnished room. I don't want to spend out my money on expensive furniture because I don't plan to live here forever. I want one furnished room, for I am going to save every penny I work here.

I just hope this paper come through soon. I don't know how much longer I can wait. I want to try and find another job that pay me my $500.00. The family I work for is nice, it's not that I dislike them, but I don't think it's fair for them to stop paying me my regular pay and only give me $400.00 a month and no explanation.

I don't really have much to complain about, except for my days off and my privacy, and you don't have that when you live in, so that is why I would like to live out when I get my landed. Some of my friends have it much harder than me. Some of the stories is hard to believe unless you in domestic work. Even though things could be better with me, I am glad the Lord lead me to Mrs. Jones and not someplace else.

"I ask the Lord to explain to the younger ones why I had to come here and work"

My other problem working with Mrs. Jones is the dog, you know walking him in the evenings. If the children get lazy and don't want to walk him, then that is my responsibility. Sometimes I end up walking it every day. The dog is old and like his own way, so when I put the leash on him, he pulling me one way and going his own way. I am not as strong as I use to be, especially because of the arthritis in my knee, so I don't like to walk him. But I don't complain. I have been here with them for a long time, and I don't want to leave, for I don't know if I would find it better out there, not with what I hear from my friends.

Sometimes the knee gives me a hard time. It hurt and hurt. The doctor said that my knee will get worse with the cold weather, so that is one of the reasons why I don't want to grow old here. At least back home my grandchildren will go and get water for me, and my children will cook a meal for me. Here in this cold country, I know there won't be anybody to do that for me. I long to see my children though, sometimes I feel like they just growing away from me. In my room I have all their pictures line up my wall.

Every night I go to bed I ask the Lord to explain to the younger ones in his own way why I had to come here and work. The older ones understand because they can see how life rough for all of us there, but sometimes it is a little harder for the younger ones to understand. I want to see them soon. I don't know how much longer this paper is going to take come through, but as soon as it come through I am going home to see them.

Hyacinth

I remember he kept pushing his finger down in my private parts and blowing hard. It really hurt, and when I told him so, he ask me if I didn't give birth to one baby already.

I met Hyacinth a year ago, through an old friend of hers, Molly, who also works as a domestic worker. Molly had been telling me for some time about her friend Hyacinth and some of the traumatic experiences she had been through, working as a live-in domestic worker in Canada.

I wanted to meet Hyacinth and Molly promised that she would try to set up a time for us all to meet, but somehow we never seemed able to get it together.

I had almost given up hope of meeting Hyacinth, when one day my doorbell rang and they were both on my steps. Hyacinth explained that she could only stay for an hour, that she had to get back to work. We tried to set up an appointment which proved to be a difficult task, because in her present job she did not get any days off. Because of this her interview took months to complete. It was often times very strenuous, reminding me of a spy movie, since we had to meet at very odd hours and in weird places.

Sometimes, I met Hyacinth in the park for half an hour or so, with her employer, but that of course was not the best way to meet, so most of the interviews took place in her little room next door to her employer's bedroom.

Sometimes it was funny, but most times, my heart was racing, keeping my fingers crossed and hoping that her employer's daughter or son would not appear, to find me with tape recorder, pen and pencil in hand. During these months, Hyacinth and I became good friends.

Hyacinth was born in the island of St. Lucia in 1956. She has been living in Canada since 1980 on an employment visa. She has one child who lives with her grandmother in St. Lucia.

When she came to Canada to work as a domestic worker, she came with high hopes, expecting to work for perhaps a year or two as a domestic worker and then go on to secretarial college. According to Hyacinth, she was in for a lot of surprises when she got here, about the country, its government and some of its people.

Hyacinth came here at the age of twenty-four years, having left St. Lucia and her little community for the first time. She came to work for a couple whom she met at one of the hotels in St. Lucia.

Hyacinth was raped by her employer within the first month of working here. He was never charged and the whole matter was treated in a hushed up way. Hyacinth had to undergo counselling with a therapist to help her deal with this trauma. Since that violent assault on her body she has left her employer and has worked with other employers, good and bad.

Presently Hyacinth works for an eighty-three-year-old woman: cleaning up after her, washing, cooking, and cleaning her huge three storey house in a well-to-do Toronto neighborhood. She is on duty twenty-four hours a day, seven days a week.

At times it was very hard for Hyacinth to talk during our interview sessions, particularly about the brutal rape that took place only a month after she came here. I reminded her that she did not have to talk about anything that would upset her, but she pushed herself and tried to remember the details. "I don't want this to happen to other girls who are coming here to work, and if I can help by telling my story I will do it."

It was hard for her to tell her story and hard for me to hear it. To know that a job could leave a woman that vulnerable, unable to speak out against assault for fear that her word would be doubted, the job lost, and deportation around the corner.

Worse yet, what happened to Hyacinth is not an isolated case.

CHILDHOOD

"I wanted so much to touch the snow"

I was about six or seven when I started hearing about England, Canada, and the United States. Is like everybody in the Caribbean talking about foreign. I remember sometimes my uncle, which is my grandmother son, use to send us old newspaper from the States and we use to read them from back to cover, what we couldn't read we ask somebody bigger to read, or just look at the pictures. I remember the first year when he was away, he would send and tell us how wonderful America was, and how you could get everything to buy. We as children use to be praying for the time when we would be big enough to travel abroad. It seem that everybody in my family lived abroad.

My own mother was in England and marry over there and had a new family. I lived in St. Lucia with my grandmother. One aunt, my mother's sister, was in Canada and my uncle and another aunt in America. Whenever they use to come home Christmas time it was always a big event to us. Is like they carry home all of America and Canada in their suitcase. The amount of pretty clothes and shoes. Boy, and the pictures, I use to look forward to those postcards of the Statue of Liberty, City Hall, and those big building and cars and the snow. I remember I just wanted so much to touch the snow.

From I was around nine, I know I was going to leave St. Lucia. I came from a large family, three brothers and myself, and lots of cousins. It was good, because you always had somebody to play with and talk secrets with, but then you know, sometimes the house was crowded. Sometimes we had to eat the same thing every day, depending on whether we got money from my mother or uncles in America. Sometimes things was a bit rough, but we was happy most of the times.

I did a little high school but I drop out, it was hard to go when the parcels from my mother stopped coming... sometimes I didn't have shoes to wear and I was too proud to go to school without shoes. Sometimes I wouldn't go to school, and other time I would borrow my cousin's shoes to wear and she would stay home from school. She would go one or two days and then I would go the other two days. But that way you miss a lot of the school, so eventually I just stop and stay home and look after my younger cousins and sometimes wash clothes for a family that live nearby.

COMING TO CANADA

"I couldn't believe my luck"

After a while I use to work as a waitress in a hotel back home. That is where I met the couple who sponsored me up here. I meet them and we talk with each other and they ask me how I would like to come up and work for them. I jump at the chance. Boy, is like my dream come true, I couldn't believe my luck. A couple months later they send my ticket with a letter saying when I come up they would take it out of my pay. This was in 1980 and I was twenty-four years old. I didn't stay with them long, only for eight months.

The first week I walked into the house the man start to bother me and want sex. I was frighten like a mouse, I didn't really expect that. When I got the job, I was suppose to look after their two little children, a girl and a boy, do the housework, wash and cook. I had my own room in the basement. It was nice, I had a T.V. and my own little bathroom in the basement. The man was a doctor, and his wife didn't really do anything. She use to leave the house in the day time but I don't know where she goes.

"He said if I had sex with him he would raise my pay"

I remember the first time I think something was funny was one night I was sleeping and I feel someone in my clothing, feeling up my private parts. This happen after I was here for a month. I jumped up because I was frighten and when I look it was him, the man I was working for. I nearly scream out, but he hold my mouth and tell me to be quiet. He smell of alcohol and I don't know where his wife was, but it was late at night. He ask me if I wasn't attracted to him, and I just look at him, I was really afraid to answer.

I remember he kept pushing his finger down in my private parts and blowing hard. It really hurt and when I told him so, he ask me if I didn't give birth to one baby already.

He tried to push me down on the bed but I wouldn't let him, and he had his hand over my mouth so I couldn't scream.

He ask me if I was going to shout, I shake my head and say no, so he let go of my mouth, I remember him telling me that if I had sex with him he would raise my pay. I tell him that I couldn't do that because he was married and his wife was upstairs. I didn't know if she was but I just say that. He laugh and ask me what Black girls know about marriage. He said some really dirty things to me. I didn't know that man had so much filth in him, and a doctor and all.

Is like it was the end of the world for me. I was so frightened... he was blowing so hard, so I could smell the alcohol strong on him. Before I know it he tear off my night clothes and he was with me right there in the bed. The more I fight the more he seem to enjoy it, so after a while I just lie down quiet and let him finish. After he finish he jump off me, spit on the floor and tell me if I tell his wife or anybody he would see that they send me back to St. Lucia or that I go to jail. I was really frightened. I really believe that I could get locked up. For what I don't know. It happened again seven or eight other times. I was just scared to say anything to anybody, further I didn't know where to turn to. I didn't know anybody here.

I didn't know where his wife was when he came to my room at nights. If she knew about it she didn't give any indication of it. Sometimes she use to stare at me, but she didn't say anything. I continue to do my work in the house — the cooking, the ironing and the cleaning — and looking after the children. There was times when I really felt ashamed, like a nobody, but I couldn't tell anybody, because there was nobody to tell about it.

Many nights I just cry, because even when I write home to my grandmother and my little boy, I had to write like everything was fine.

"I was scared to tell Immigration"

As time goes by and I take the children to the park, I start to notice that there was another West Indian girl who always was in the park with children. So one day I says good morning to her and we start to talk. I got to know that she just lived around the corner from me and that she was in the same line of work. We start to talk, and I get to like her and she like me, and of course we talk about the people we work for. One day I tell her what was going on with me at the house and she tell me that I could go to Immigration to complain and that I could look for another job. I was scared, because I thought that maybe they would deport me.

She promise to come down with me, and she did, but she didn't come in with me. She wait close outside at a restaurant for me. I go in and tell my story. I think I tell it six different times to six different officers. They wanted to know everything. I felt so cheap talking to them, they wanted to hear every little detail of what *really* happen with me and the doctor. That was the Friday and they said I was to get back in touch with them the Monday morning. I don't know what happen, but when I go home the evening is like all hell break loose. I never know that Immigration work so fast. When I go in I get one big cussing from his wife. She call me ungrateful-jealous-slut-black-bitch. I can't even remember some of the words. She said, "If you and Don had a problem why didn't you come to me? Why Immigration? We could have worked it out." Then she started shouting again and calling me black bitch. I just run to my room and scream down the place. I was scared. Before I know it his wife just come into my room, open the door without knocking and started slapping me up, telling me that is me bring sex argument to her husband, and that we "nigger girls" are good for nothing else, and asking me if I like it when her husband have sex with me. I was crying the whole time, because I wasn't use to this treatment. Then she tell me I had to leave her house. So I pack up my little things and went and stay with my friend.

When I go down to Immigration the Monday morning they told me that I could go and look another job, but that I shouldn't waste any time fooling around. The man that I talk to never even ask me if I felt sick with what happened, or if I went to see a doctor, not one word about what happened to me.

"I got a job with a nice lady"

Well, I look day and night after that for a job, but I was scared. If I went to a house for an interview and saw the husband, I just started to think about what happened to me. Eventually I got a job with a nice lady, she's a lawyer and she has two children. I was glad when that came through, because time was running out on me and I didn't want the Immigration to start bugging me, plus my girlfriend's place where I was staying was just one room. I didn't want to be a burden to her because she was good to me. You know how it is, sometimes you have a friend and you depend on them so much that they just get tired of you. I spent about a year and a half working for the lawyer. She help me a lot. She even help to find me a lady therapist, someone who I could talk to about what happened to me. It really help me a lot.

There was a time when I would just start to tremble when a man come around me, or if I was in a place alone with them. So I was glad that this lady help me to find the therapist.

The children had manners to me. I had my own room with a little colour T.V., a bed and a dresser, my own bathroom. In my work, I was responsible for the children. I take them to nursery school, I wash clothes, clean the house, cook for the children, and then pick them up from school. Most of the time I didn't cook for the lady because she usually eats out. She didn't bother me in the evening to find out what I did all day, and I met a lot of girls who tell me that this happen to them. The only thing about the job that I didn't like was the hours; because she was a lawyer, sometimes I would have to work later than my usual 7:00 p.m. depending on if she comes home or not. Sometimes she will not call home, so I might make arrangements to see one of my friends or go somewhere and have to cancel it. And then again sometimes on weekends — which is suppose to be my time off — I might have to work because she had to go out of town. So it use to restrict me. Sometimes, if I work later than my hours or if I work on weekends, or say when she go out of town for two weeks, she would pay me a bit extra. But I liked working for her. She would tell me that I have a good life ahead of me, and she even helped me to get into a typing course at George Brown.

What I find is that the first time I went down to Employment (Manpower) and Immigration and told them that I wanted to do upgrading for my landed they try to get me to take a course in Health Care Aide. I didn't want to do that, I wanted to do the typing course, but they wouldn't listen to me. Well, the lady I work for called them up and talk to them. One day she went down with me to Manpower and tell them that typing was what I said I wanted to do. So they let me register.

Well, you know, it's like good things never last long, she was from the States and her mother and father was killed in a plane crash and she had to go back there to look after their business and their land. I was sad to see her and the children go because she really help me a lot.

"I am just sticking it out until I get my landed"

Well, when she left I had to find another job, which is the job I am in now and boy, if I could leave it tomorrow I would. I'm working for another lady and I tell you it makes me cry some nights when I think of this life. I only took this job because time was running out and the Immigration was bothering me about finding another job soon.

The lady I work for is eighty-two years old. The minute I walk in and saw the situation, I knew that I wouldn't like it. First I don't know if is the old lady's fault, maybe not, maybe all old white people in Canada like this. I just know that in St. Lucia I know old people that age who is strong and healthy. Well, this is a big house and is only the lady and me. Her husband died about a year ago, so she is very lonely for him, because they were married for over fifty years.

My room is right next to her. I don't get any sleep at nights, because she begins to wake up all hours of the night and keep calling for me, "Hyacinth, Hyacinth." Then I have to get up and go and hold her hand. Or if she don't call for me, she call out for "George! George!", the name of her husband. I have to get up early in the morning around 6:00 or so, is like she hardly sleep.

When I got the job, about five months ago, her daughter told me that I was just to look after her mother, cook her supper and be beside her, and take her for walks in her wheelchair, when it is nice out. But after I was there for around a month, I hear from her son, that the cleaning lady is sick and I must take over that job, so now I find I cook, take her for her walks, read to her, clean her up when she mess up herself, clean the house and wash the clothes, do the grocery shopping all at the same time, and not for any more money.

Right now I get $710.00 a month, which is what I am suppose to get as Manpower say. But when I took the job, I wasn't told that I was suppose to clean and wash clothes too for that money. I am afraid to go and complain to Manpower, because this is my third job, and they watch this sort of thing, so maybe if I go and complain they might tell me to go home. They might think I am a trouble-maker. I am just sticking it out until I get my landed. But it is very hard work. Sometimes, Mrs. Horowitz dumb, and when she wants to go to the bathroom, she would just go in her clothes, without calling me. When I talk to her son about getting another lady to do the house cleaning and the laundry, he pretend that he don't hear me. Sometimes she falls off the bed and I have to lift her up. After I do that, I feel all kinds of pain in my back because she is heavy.

I wish I could just come out of domestic work. I know for sure that this is not something I want to do forever. Right now I don't know what is going to happen with my upgrading, because I have to look after Mrs. Horowitz all day and all night and I can't get to go to my classes. I talked to her daughter about it and she said she would try to work out something, but it is going on three weeks now and she don't say anything to me, and so now I am missing my classes.

The government say your employer is suppose to give you time off to do the course but I'm not getting that.

I know three girls that already get deported this year, and it wasn't even their fault one girl was changing her job for the second time in six years and they deported her, I really believe that it was because of how many children she had back home. She has about seven children back home, and I believe that the government don't want to land women who have more than two or the most three children back home.

I hear from a lot of the girls in domestic work that the government trying to keep out the old domestics and the domestics with too many children. So I think that if I get to finish this typing course I might have a good chance to get my landed because I just have one child. I don't think it's fair though for the government to do that to people who have lots of children.

"I feel like an old woman"

If I get my landed, I'd send for him the next day, because I want him to get a good education, and also I long to see him. Sometimes I wonder if he will remember me. My grandmother send me pictures of him. I have them stick up all over my wall in my room.

It's so sad how we girls have to leave our children behind for so long, just so that we can work and make a little money to put food in their stomach.

You know, I'm not even thirty years old yet, and I feel like an old woman. When I look at Canadian girls my age, and see how happy and carefree they are, I wonder why it is so hard for Black people. Is like we born to suffer.

When I get this landed I want to bring my grandmother up for a visit. I don't think she would want to live here, she like it in St. Lucia, but I would like her to come up and know Canada. You know, she has helped me so much, with my little son and even when I was growing up she was like my own mother.

Every day I look in the mailbox or I listen on T.V. to see if there is anything new about domestic workers. I want to get that landed very much.

Why is it people take so much liberty with you just because you live in their homes? My life now is like a prison. I am not joking. I don't get any days off. I work from Monday to Monday. The only time I get to go outside is when I take Mrs. Horowitz for a walk, otherwise I am in the house or in the backyard when I wheel her outside.

"Sometimes I wonder if her daughter and son have any feelings"

You know, sometimes I sit and wonder if her daughter or son have any feelings. When they come to visit her they don't even ask me about myself. All they want to know about is if she vomit today, or if she acting weird, you know like calling out for her husband in the nights. They hardly even sit and talk with her. I am the one who do all that, and yet when they come and see the dirty clothes pile up, they quarrel and ask me what I have been doing all week. No feelings for me. Is like I am a machine or something.

I don't really have any friends any more. One or two of my friends still call sometimes, but not that much, because I can never get time off to go out with them. I can't leave this job until my papers come through. It is too near for me to get my landed. I can't leave now, because they might deport me, this is what I hear from other girls. But, I just don't know how much longer I can stick out this job. I know I can't stay here for another twelve months under these conditions.

"This is no life for a person"

I pray every night for this landed to come through, I never work so hard in my life. I came to this country with a lot of high hopes — going to school, finishing up, and maybe even going to college but all that seem to be gone. Now I find myself crying all the time, and sometimes I just think that I won't be able to survive — last out this wait until the landed.

This kind of life is not for me. This is no life for a person. Sometimes when I remember how much I use to laugh back home, I wonder if I am the same person. For all I seems to do now is cry.

I think it is a terrible thing when people like me have to go through so much just to make a living.

Molly

I wish I could have my family here with me — loneliness — it makes you feel so helpless, so vulnerable, so ashamed. It's almost like a crime.

I first met Molly at a Jamaican Canadian Association Domestic Workers' meeting in the winter of 1981. She was one of the first women who agreed to be a part of *SILENCED*. Her enthusiasm was overwhelming. I remembered that within minutes of meeting each other, she pressed a scrap of paper with her phone number in my hand and told me to call her the next day to set up a time to meet.

On my way to Molly's house, I experienced feelings of doubt. I wondered if she'd be home, or whether she'd changed her mind and decided not to go through with it again. But I had nothing to worry about, because when I knocked at her door, Molly answered.

Molly lives in a three-storied rooming house in a working class neighborhood of downtown Toronto. She shares a kitchen and bath with four other persons, and occupies a room on the third floor. Her small room holds a bed, a 12" black and white television set and her baby's crib. Molly has decorated her small room with photographs of her children, tourist posters of Jamaica and crocheted sets on top of her dresser drawers and on the window sill. She asks my opinion of the room. I tell her it feels comfortable. She agrees, but whispers to me that she wishes she didn't have to share the bathroom and the kitchen. She says that she hopes she'll be able to move to a larger place when she gets her landed status.

You know, with a little baby here in the room with me there isn't much space and he's growing fast, he needs space to move around, for here is not like Jamaica where he can go outside a lot.

Molly is a tall statuesque woman in her late thirties. She is very religious and attends church almost every Sunday. She has been working in Canada for the past nine years as a domestic on the Employment Visa.

She is not shy about talking into a tape recorder. She talks rapidly and each word is filled with determination. There is an air of openness and warmth in her voice as she talks about her teenage years, her children and her work here in Canada as a domestic worker.

Here is Molly's story:

TEENAGE YEARS

"Ever since I can remember life was rough"

I started working on the work permit in 1978, but that was not the first time I came to Canada. The first time was in 1973, but I was on the go. [1] The idea to come to Canada was really started with my friend. We were really good friends in Jamaica, we went everywhere together. We even had our babies around the same time. Well, she and I use to always talk about coming to Canada as tourists and then staying on to work as domestics.

Things were not really working out for us in Jamaica. Most of the time we couldn't find work and we had our children to feed and send to school. Ever since I can remember life was rough for me, even as a girl growing up. We grew up in the country, a place called St. Thomas, but I left St. Thomas when I was about fourteen years old. I went to Kingston to stay with an aunt and to find work. I didn't even finish high school. [2] My family couldn't afford to school all of us, especially us girls. But I was glad not to have to go to school because I use to have to walk barefoot for about six miles back and forth every day. It was really embarrassing, especially when we had to pass boys on the way.

When first I went to Kingston I stayed with my aunt and I worked with a lady looking after her children and cleaning and cooking for her. When I was about sixteen years old I met my boyfriend who I have my children for and eventually I moved out of my aunt to live with him. I had some really bad times in Kingston, trying to find work, making enough money for my family to live on. Sometimes it got really rough. I remember I use to just sit and cry some days when I couldn't find the money to buy food for my children. My boyfriend wasn't working most of the times and so everybody depended on me. That's when I decided to come to Canada.

My girlfriend had another friend who was a domestic worker in Montreal and she eventually left Jamaica to go there. A few months after she left I bought my ticket as a tourist and came to Toronto. This was in 1973. When I came to Immigration they questioned me for over an hour and finally they let me through and I went and found a hotel to sleep that night. The next morning I got somebody to direct me to the bus station and I took the Gray Coach bus to Montreal. I was all alone by myself and I felt frightened. But when I got to Montreal I asked questions and then took a taxi to where my friend was living. I didn't stay with her for long. I felt a bit shy staying with her because I didn't know her friend that she was staying with, and then she wasn't adjusted to the place so we didn't get on the same way we did in Jamaica. I wasn't happy in Montreal and it was hard to find work because I don't speak French. Soon after that I met another Jamaican girl in Montreal and I became friends with her. She told me her mother lived around Dufferin and King Street in Toronto and she asked me if I wanted to come to Toronto with her. I said yes.

"The work was hard, the hours long and the pay lousy"

We came back together and I stayed with her and her mother for a while. They were very nice to me. Whenever my friend got jobs for herself, she would take one and give me one. Once she got me a job with some people, but I didn't stay there long because the people didn't want to pay me and sometimes I didn't even get enough to eat. So I just stayed there a little while and then I left.

Eventually I meet some new friends through this same girlfriend of mine. I remember one of my new friends was doing a job around Richmond Hill [3] for about $25.00 a week and she decided to give it to me because she found a better job. You know something, when I started working with this lady she never paid me the full $25.00. She knew I wasn't landed, that I wasn't on a work permit, that I was here illegally and that I couldn't complain to anybody — so she just kept on giving me the $20.00 a week. I work hard for that money -- cleaning the floors, washing dishes, washing clothes and looking after two young children. I was living-in so I was like on call twenty-four hours a day.

By 1974 I was disgusted and fed up of that kind of life, hiding from Immigration, not being able to speak up for my rights. Plus I was feeling very lonely. I was missing my boyfriend and my three children. (Right now my children are thirteen, twelve and ten years old. I send money for them regularly, but oh God, I miss them. When I left in 1973 my youngest child was nine months old. I know that whenever we meet again he won't even know me. It hurts.) But I knew that I couldn't go home because maybe I wouldn't be so lucky the next time coming through Immigration. So again I left that job and tried to find something in a little better condition. I put ads in the paper to find another job, but I got so much crank calls that I had to take the ads out.

A friend of mine who was working at Mayfair Mansion told me they were looking for people and to apply. I got the job and stayed there for about a year and some weeks. I eventually left there too. It was the same story — the work was hard and the hours was long and the pay lousy. When I left Mayfair I got another little cleaning job to do — go around to different offices at night and clean. The company use to take us out on cleaning jobs. But sometimes for two weeks, we only got $40.00 a week. Sometimes you might go there every day for the two weeks and you might go on a cleaning job for only three nights. So you end up wasting a lot of time sitting around waiting to see if they will call you. The thing is you had to go there every night and sit and wait to see if any cleaning jobs come in. But I think they had their favourites who they give the jobs to. Boy, with that job, I thought I was going out of my mind because there was just not enough money.

"I had an aim in view"

Eventually I met a friend who worked at a hospital in Toronto who told me about a patient who was going home and needed somebody to look after her. She told me she would make the arrangements for me. She did and I went on the interview.

I remember it was a Sunday and she kind of nervous with me, I guess because she was alone and an old woman. I eventually start to work with her from March 1976, then I went back home in 1978 and she applied to Manpower and Immigration and took me back legally on a work permit. I stayed and worked with her until she died in August 1981. She was eighty-three years old when she died. I really missed her. Of course, we did have our little misunderstanding through the years that I work with her, but I tell you, of all the people I worked with, she was the best.

I use to get $118.00 a week. It could have been more, but I was satisfied. I figured it was only her alone that I had to look after and you know it wasn't that much work. I didn't wash for her. Her clothes went to the laundry, except for those she soiled up which I washed. I cooked for her and I did the dusting around the house. There was another lady who came in once a week to do the heavy house cleaning. So the hardest thing really was changing her clothes when she eventually became incontinent. But I was very grateful for the job and the $118.00 a week. Like I said, she was a nice lady and in a lot of ways, I was more like a companion to her. She had a lot of nieces and nephews but they did not visit her a lot. I remember her niece use to say to me that she doesn't know how I stand her aunt. None of her nieces ever stayed longer than fifteen minutes with her. Sometimes she acted kind of weird and I guess they were frightened. She use to make a lot of noises like " whoo, whoo, whooooooo" day and night. Sometimes, I had to close my door and my room was right in front of her's so closing the door didn't block out the noise. But I had an aim in view, so I didn't get fed up and leave the job. Not that I was using the job or her as a convenience. But I knew what I wanted and she needed me. Both of us needed each other. She had no children and her husband had died twenty-one years ago. So it was just the two of us in the house and then later my little baby.

Her friends and relatives hardly came to see her. They said that she was too miserable and that every time they came there all they could hear about was how sick she was so they kept away from her. During those times I was the closest one to her. I was a companion to her. I listened to her when she talked. Read to her. Brush her hair for her. Made sure she took her medication. Fed her, you know — things like that. But it comes a time about six months before she died when she became incontinent. She did everything in bed. So I had to do everything for her then. Like tidy her off, clean up the bed, just be around her whenever she wanted me. The housekeeper still came in once a week, but otherwise I had to do everything for her. You know, it was probably all those things, like lifting her onto the bed when she fell was why I had to eventually go in the hospital with a hernia — I had to lift her so many times.

One of the reasons why I really liked Mrs. Tucker and put up with all of that during the last months was because she really gave me the chance to get on the work permit. Plus when I came back on the work permit in 1978 I was three months pregnant which I didn't tell her because I was afraid that if she found out she wouldn't hire me. But when she found out, she didn't run me from the job.

Boy, I really went through a lot in this country. I remember the night when I set in to have the baby. I remember when the pain took me I was in her room. I had to kneel down on the floor at her bedside because pain was really so awful. I remember I told her I had to go to the hospital. She phoned her minister and told him that I fainted. When I got to the hospital she phoned and they told her that I had a little baby boy. Looking back on it now, I can't really see how she didn't see that I was pregnant. She could see and she could hear pretty good, but she was conveniently deaf and blind when she wanted to. After I had the baby, I came out of the hospital and I continued to look after Mrs. Tucker and I brought the baby home with me. Mrs. Tucker was still a little shocked when I came home with the baby, but still she overcome that. She get to — not admit — she get to accept it. As a matter of fact she even named the baby.

"I needed a job or they would deport me"

After she passed away I had to find another job. The next job I got was the worst job I have ever had from I come to Canada. It was a job working at a home for ex-mental patients. I didn't know anything about my employer or the job when I took the job. Time was running out on me, my visa was going to be expired and so I needed to be in a job or they would deport me. This was September 1981 and my visa would run out by October 1981. Mrs. Tucker was dead and I needed to have a job. That job was really awful. Working with Mrs. Tucker during the last months of her life was one hundred per cent better than this last job. So that should show you how bad it was. This woman (the new employer) didn't respect people who worked with her. She treated everybody like a dog.

I remember that I took sick the sixth month I was working with this new woman. I was sick with a hernia problem and I had to go into the hospital. They told me that I had to get surgery in my belly button. This was the pain that had been hurting me on and off for the past two years since I was with Mrs. Tucker. The night I took in with the hernia I was on the job and I was scared. Before it would always hurt and stop. Sometimes it use to hurt and then it would swell big — big like a rock —but then it would always go right back in after I put hot water on it. This time the pain started from the Tuesday and by Thursday, I couldn't even take the street car home. I had to get a friend to take me to the doctor. He told me it was bad and that I should go to the emergency section of the Doctors' Hospital. Boy, I'm telling you, I would never like to go through all that pain again — it was kind of horrible. Because I was to have surgery, I had to stay in the hospital for a couple of days. Well, on the third day that I was in the hospital, I heard that my employer got another girl to fill my vacancy. It was two of us girls who always work in the home. So on the third day she got another new girl. She didn't even say anything to me and she knew where I was. I stayed six days in the hospital. When I came out I spoke to Mrs. Smith, my employer, on the telephone and she didn't ask me to come back. She didn't say anything to me about the job. She didn't say anything. I was so hurt. It was as if she use me and I am of no more service so forget about me and find somebody else to do the job.

Let me tell you about my job with her for the six months. There were two of us who usually work there at the house. We were in charge of the thirty patients. And one of us usually had to sleep over with them. Mrs. Smith hardly ever came down to the house unless to supervise or complain about something we did wrong. The house was a very big house — it had three floors. Some of the rooms had four to five beds each. The patients all ate downstairs in the basement. There were about five tables down there and then there were bathrooms on each floor. We had to do almost everything in that house — cook, clean, wash, scrub the floors, give the patients their medication. You name it — we had to do it. It was dreadful like hell there. It was very tense in the house because a lot of the patients are ex-mental patients from 999[4] and sometimes if they didn't take their medication they could get violent and attack us. We had to be calling the police almost every day. They (the police) use to tell us that what we are doing is a man's job. They use to say that a man should be there with us. But because Mrs. Smith didn't want to pay out the extra money, she only had us two girls there to do all the work every day.

I use to get $85.00 a week. I was going off my head because that job just couldn't support me and the baby. I was boarding him out for $50.00 a week, plus I still had to send money for my three children back home. So because of that I had to take up another job too. I was at the boarding house from eight in the morning to around seven at night. Then I would go to another cleaning job from nine at night to six in the morning. I use to get no sleep. I tell you I was going crazy. But I had to keep it up because I had to be paying out so much bills. I was hardly saving any money because I had to send home money too. Plus the $50.00 for the baby, plus pay my rent. Sometimes I had to even sleep over at the boarding house. That was when the other girl who live-in had her days off and Mrs. Smith wanted somebody there for the weekend.

I remember there was a high turnover of girls there at the home. Girls use to quit every two weeks or so, but as soon as they quit Mrs. Smith would find somebody else to take their place. Nobody stayed at that place very long. They quit as fast as they come. And there's always other girls to fill their vacancy. This is why when I got sick she didn't care whether I came back or not, because she knew she could get another girl with no problem.

Even now she have money for me I remember I went into the hospital the Thursday evening and I was suppose to get paid the Friday, and until now — it's three months now — I haven't got my money from her yet. I phoned her and told her I need my money and still I haven't got it yet I phoned and left a message with the new girl that is working there. I said to her, "Please tell Mrs. Smith to leave my money. I will come and pick it up." She hasn't left my money yet. I really need the money because I need it to look after my little boy here and my three children in Jamaica.

The other day I was telling a friend of mine about Mrs. Smith and the meagre salary she was paying me. My friend was asking how she manage to get away with it from Manpower. But the thing is, Manpower don't know because she told Manpower she was paying me $100.00 a week. It's on the paper, it's written down in the contract. When I started working with her she told me she was paying me $85.00 a week. She is a crook and she thinks she is smart. She thinks I don't know. But I knew what was going on. She is so ungrateful. She knew she was paying me less than I'm suppose to get. And because I get off and have to go to the hospital she get someone else. She didn't even care if I eat or have a place to live.

I'm telling you, in a way I'm glad she didn't ask me to come back. I don't want anything else to do with that woman. All I want from her now is my money. I just want to forget about her.

"We're doing the dirty work"

Some employers are good and some don't care much about you. All they want to do is work you like a slave and as soon as anything happen to you, whether on the job or not, that's it. That's it. They want no part of you. But thank God, all of them are not the same because Mrs Tucker wasn't like that. I'm not expecting all of them to be the same, but show a little gratitude. Show your appreciation. We're doing the dirty work. They are paying the money. But they think probably we are nobody. They must treat us equal, like we are human beings too, not like some animal. My experience with Mrs. Smith make me feel very bitter.

Well, I'm going to put an ad in the papers Friday, Saturday and Sunday. I don't know if it will help but I would really like to get another job soon. Maybe I'll even have to take one live-in. I don't like those jobs, though. It's not nice living-in at peoples' houses. They don't treat us with any kindness or understanding. Sometimes, what they give us to eat is not even sufficient, not even nourishing. The other thing is that we doesn't have privacy in the houses. They come and knock us up every time they can't find something no matter what time it is. We have to be right there until they fall asleep. These things are not fair.

It would be nice if we were allowed to rent a room on our own. Some of us would feel better about domestic work if we could come out of their home and go home to our home. It's really not nice the way they treat us. We don't have much choice because you come from your country and you don't know anybody here. After you are here a little time and you have friends, Manpower and Immigration should allow you to rent a place of your own. Because after you are here a little time and you make friends, then you want your own social life. You want to work in the days and go home in the nights like anybody else.

Some of us have been here four, five, six years and still living in peoples' basements or sharing rooms with small children. I know people who are stuck in peoples' houses for eight years. My God. I really feel sorry for them. Most of them can't take their friends there. You have no social life, and if you even go out for Sunday, by Sunday night you have to be back in. It's not really lovely.

"Just half way through my journey, I still have another half to go"

I'm just praying I get a job soon and that it is a job that I can live-out. If not, I'll have to take a live-in. Right now, I pay $130.00 a month for this room and I share the kitchen and bathroom with someone else. I feel a little more comfortable having my own room and having my privacy. If I had my landed, though, I would feel much better because then I could go any place. I could look any job I wanted. Even now, we are not allowed to take factory jobs, only domestic work.[5]

I'm just crossing my fingers that I will get my landed soon. I apply for landed status but I don't hear anything. I'm just counting the months. I miss my children but I can't go down to look for them until I get my landed. I wish I could have them here with me — loneliness — it's almost like a crime. It makes you feel so, so helpless. so vulnerable, so ashamed. It's almost like a crime. The only socialising I really do is go to church. Right now, I'm involved in this domestic workers group and so we meet once a month. That really comes in handy because it eases the loneliness.

Sometimes when I talk to some of my girlfriends, I tell them to try to join a church group or the Domestic Workers' Group, but a lot of them don't take this advice. We just prefer to stay in our own little small world by ourselves, we don't want to get involved. But I keep telling them that if they don't go out, they won't know what's going on. Like the last time I went down to Immigration, they kept asking me if I belonged to any church or group. I think they ask you those things because they want to know if anything happens to you how you are going to manage. But a lot of girls are kind of confused. Are we suppose to join groups or are we not suppose to? Some girls believe if you join a group you might make it bad for yourself. They feel that maybe the Immigration won't like this.

I just hope that I get this landed. They say it would take about a year. I'm praying I get it soon. It's been a real struggle, believe me. But I made up my mind to stick it out because I've gone a long way and I can't turn back now. It's hard in Jamaica for a lot of people. That why we come here and even when we come here there is still the hardship. Sometimes you don't even know who to trust. I have this friend who hired a lawyer and the lawyer charged her $800.00 just to go down to Immigration with her. She is on a work permit and she applied once for landed and they turned her down. I don't know why she needs a lawyer because she could apply on her own. Boy, $800.00 just for him to take her down one time to say three little words.

Right now, I'm trying to get into George Brown College to take a course in Health Care Aide. In order to get your landed they want you to show them a certificate of some kind. Usually when you go down to Immigration to apply to do the course they want to dig deep down in your background. And you don't even know what they want to know.

Each part of the course cost $70.00 and there are about six different parts. The course really cost $35.00, but because they're charging us foreign student rate I have to pay $70.00 for each part.

Like I said, life here in Canada has been a real struggle. But I just make up my mind to stick it out because I've been a long way since I came here first in 1973. When I finish this course at George Brown and get the certificate that means I can go and work in any institution — like a hospital or look after the elderly. I wouldn't want to stay in domestic work when I finish school and get my landed. No way. I would get out of it so fast that nobody would believe it.

When I get my landed I would like to send for the kids and my boyfriend. He does construction work back home and I know he would get a job if he came up. I'd be so happy because I wouldn't have to hustle so much, because I've been doing a lot of it in this country. All by myself. Sometimes I feel tired. I need some help. I says to myself, if he were here, I wouldn't even have to think of looking for a job right away. I could stay home with the baby for a while. Now that I board him out, I hardly see him — only on weekends. I just hope everything work out fine and I get the landed and my family get to come up. I want to start living like a normal person with my family.

"Just to feel more free"

It's been such a hard struggle with the Immigration. I only hope they don't reject my application. It would be so nice to feel free. Not that I am not free, because I don't feel like a criminal, but just to feel more free. Free to go anywhere I want to go. Free to look for any kind of job I want. God, I just hope something might come through quick. I've been struggling for so long that sometimes I wonder if it will ever end or if this is to be my life. It seems so long.

It's not easy I tell you, leaving your country and coming to this country to work. It's not easy. But if you leave your country with a dream, you just have to make up your mind that you want that dream to come through some day. You know, a lot of us come here as illegal immigrants and we are not free. We are like prisoners and we hide and hope that one day we will be like normal human beings.

I was like that once too, and now, thank God, I'm not one hundred per cent free, but I know now that I don't have to hide. I can open the door if the doorbell rings. When I walk on the street I don't have to keep looking back unless I expect someone. I don't have to look for a police car or look at anybody funny. When I was here the first time without the permit, I felt terrified and a lot of times I felt like dying. You know, like when you hear the doorbell and don't know whether to answer it or not. I'm telling you, it can really wrack your nerves.

But, like I always say, things and time have a way of working out itself and sometimes you just have to wait on time. Just be patient. I have been waiting for the past nine years in this country and I'm just half way there. Just half way through my journey, I still have another half to go.

I don' t know when it will I end, but I am still going hang in there because I still have hopes and I feel I've been through the worst.

Myrtle

It's really hard ... working for somebody and looking after their
children, because every day it's a reminder of your own children ...
But I couldn't stay home and see my children suffer.

Myrtle is a fifty-four year old woman who came to Canada twelve years
ago from Dominica. She has eight children in Dominica who she supports
singlehandedly.

To date she has worked in this country as a chambermaid and a domestic
worker.

At fifty-four years old, she is perhaps one of the oldest women on the
Employment Visa. Myrtle presently works with a family of six and has been
with them since 1974. Myrtle says that the work is strenuous and the hours
long. "Sometimes I feel tired in the nights, because the children mess up the
house and I have to clean up after them." Myrtle is aware of her age and
knows that if she leaves this job before she receives landed status it could
work against her, so she's sticking it out.

Her youngest daughter is ten years old, and the last time she saw her she
was twelve months old. She wonders when next she'll see her again.

Most of all Myrtle is worried about her future. She suffers from arthritis in
her knees, and she finds that some days it is almost impossible to get through
the washing, cooking, cleaning, ironing and childcare activities. Myrtle is
deeply religious and as she says, "The Lord Jesus makes me forget all my
troubles.... "

This is Myrtle's story:

WORKING IN CANADA

"The money at home wasn't enough to support my family"

I am fifty-four years old. I came to Toronto twelve years ago. Sometimes
it looks like I only came yesterday. What I mean is that I hardly know
anywhere. I don't really go out, ever since I came here it was from work to
home, and now is just from church to home. Since I have been here I have
never even gone to a movie. I don't know what a movie house look like
inside.

When I came to Canada in 1971, I wasn't on the work permit. I came up
here on a invitation letter from a friend who was here working as a domestic.
She write to me in Dominica and told me that she was working as a
babysitter and that if I came up it wouldn't be hard for me to get a job. I was
glad for the break, because I wasn't doing anything in Dominica. It was hard

to find work, and when I did work the money wasn't enough to support my family. I have eight children back home in Dominica, and I am the only one looking after them. My youngest is ten years old. The last time I see her she was twelve months old.

In 1971, I came up to my friend and I stayed with her for a while, and I got a job as a chambermaid in a hotel. They didn't ask me for any papers and I was glad for that. It took me about three weeks to find that job. Some places wanted papers, but this place didn't want any so I started working there.

The work was hard and dirty. I stayed it out for a year before I left. I had to leave, not that I wanted to; because out of that money I could send home a little something for my children. But I was given the dirtiest rooms to clean. I began to notice that sometimes when I'm going through four rooms some of the other women working there were just finishing up their first room. They were there longer so I guess they knowed how to operate. Is like they try to break in new girls by giving them the dirtiest rooms to clean and the longest shifts. I even began to notice that I was not getting pay for my overtime and for the holidays that I worked. I remember one day I ask the supervisor about it and she asked me to bring in my papers for her to see. When I got home and told my friend about it, she told me that I mustn't go back to the job, because the supervisor was going to squeal on me. She told me that those hotel people know that most of the girls working there wasn't landed and so they try and overwork them because they know they couldn't go to the law.

"Sometimes when I work two shifts, they only pay me for one"

I left that job and tried to get one in a factory, but I walk until my foot was tired, everywhere I was told the same thing, that I need Canadian experience. Yet when I worked as a chambermaid nobody ask me for Canadian experience. I walk and answer a lot of ads in the paper and every time I go for the job interview they said that the job was taken.

Eventually, I went back to work in another hotel as a chambermaid. I told them I had experience working as a chambermaid because I thought they would give me more money, but they didn't. They pay me the same pay, minimum wage; and when I worked holidays, they never pay me overtime, sometimes even when I work two shifts they only pay me for the one I work. But I was scared to speak up so I didn't. Eventually I save up my money and bought a suitcase and every week I went to Honest Ed's and bought clothes for my children. Then I bought a barrel at one of the West Indian stores and buy more shoes and clothes and flour and rice, and when the barrel and the suitcase was pack with clothes and food, I bought a ticket and went home.

I couldn't take it here any longer, this wasn't the kind of life I was accustom to.

"I wait day and night for the letter"

So I went back home around the beginning of 1973, but that didn't last long. I didn't stay there for long because things was just the same, nothing had changed at all. Life was still hard, and when the flour and rice was finished we all was back to stage one. No money, no work, no food.

Well, is like God was on my side. I had another friend working up here at the time, and she wrote to me and tell me that she knows a lady looking for someone to take care of her children. She send the lady name and address and I ask one of my elder daughters to help me write the letter and I mail it the same day to the lady in Canada. I wait day and night for the letter.

A month later it came. She wanted me to send my picture, my age and how early I could leave Dominica. It took me about two months to answer her because you know Dominica is not like here where it is cheap to take pictures and get them back the same day. Money is hard over there, and I wanted to take a nice picture at a studio to send to her. One of my friends back in Dominica said that I should lie about my age because maybe she wouldn't want to take me up. But I didn't see any reason to do that, so I wrote and tell her my true age, but I told her that I was strong and that I have never been sick and that I can clean and cook and look after children good. So thank God, she arrange for the work permit and I came back up the beginning of 1974.

Well, now I'm still working for the same lady, sometimes the work is hard, and most times I don't get my days off when I am suppose to get it, but thank God, I am still in a job. At my age you can't be too choosy, especially how I am on the work permit, it wouldn't take anything much for the government to deport me, send me back home to Dominica.

"Sometimes I feel tired in the nights"

The lady I work with has four children, and I look after them. I do everything for them, you name it. The lady work in a office, I don't know what she do in there and her husband work as a manager in one of the major supermarket. Like I said they don't treat me bad, I have a room in the basement and my own bathroom. The only thing that I don't like is that the dog sleep in the basement too. He is not in my room but he sleep down there, and you know, he's old and sick and sometimes he howls late at night and wake me up. I don't say anything about that, because everybody love him, he is the pet and he was there from before I came there to work.

I also wash all the clothes for the family, and clean the house, you know, vacuum and dust, and I look after the children meals. Mrs. Jones, looks after her husband food in the evenings, and they look after their own breakfast in the mornings. So it's the children I look after mostly.

Sometimes I feel tired in the nights, because the children mess up the house and I have to clean up after them, wash up after them. Sometimes the big girl who is thirteen help me with the dishes and if she is in a good mood she help me with the vacuum too. She is nice and treat me with respect. The other boy is eight and then there is a girl six years old. The other boy is four years old. He is like the baby and spoiled. I always have to pick up after him and get things for him. And sometimes my temper raise so high I want to just hit him, but that don't happen all the while because I try to keep my temper under control.

I bought a little television last Christmas because the black and white one that I had in my room needed fixing. So out of my saving I bought a nice little twelve-inch black and white. Sometimes the big girl come to my room and watch T.V. with me. Like I said we get on most times, so she'll come and talk to me about school, her boyfriends, and sometimes even if she and her mother have words, she'll come and cry in my room. She is a really sweet girl.

"If I didn't have to I wouldn't be here"

She reminds me of my children. Lord only know how much I miss them. All I have of them is pictures for memories. It's really hard you know, working for somebody and looking after their children because every day it's a reminder of your own children.

I know a lot of people say that we shouldn't come here and leave our children back home, but what else can we do? Our children have to eat. You can't talk to some people about things like that because they don't know what it is like to live in a one room with seven other people, all sleeping on one bed and some on the floor. It's hard. If I didn't have to, I wouldn't be here. But I couldn't stay home and see my children suffer. At least working here, I can send home money and clothes for them.

I don't know when I will see them again, how soon it will be. I apply to get my landed but I don't hear anything yet from the government. Right now I am doing a Health Care Aide course at George Brown College, I just praying that I will pass the course so that my landed will be easy to get.

I get so tired you know, is like a long slow journey on a bus. I am tired, I want to get off this journey. I don't really know what I am going to do when I get my landed. Sometimes I think that I might just stay in domestic work, for it's the only thing I really know how to do. I don't think I would live-in, though. I want a place of my own no matter how small it is. But I think I will continue domestic work, maybe work for different people, I think I could make more money that way, and I wouldn't have to spend a whole day in somebody house. Just go there, clean up the house, wash, iron, pick up my money and then leave. Babysitting is out. I am too tired for that, and children take a lot out of you. So I will just clean and wash and then go home to my house.

You know what worries me sometimes is what going to happen to me in years from now. I worry about old age security and things like that, because I don't know anything about those things and I wonder, what will happen to me then. I don't even know how long I can keep up this cleaning. I have arthritis in my right knee and sometimes when I kneel down too long on it, I get pain from it. Sometimes it can last for days and then it swells up. I wonder what will happen to me when I can't use my knee any longer. Is things like this that make me worry sometimes about if I will get my landed or not.

I don't know what I would do if I went back home. I give Canada twelve good years. I came and work in this country and tried to live up to the law of the country, so I hope they look at those things when they judge my file. There is nothing for me to do if I go back home. If this knee continue to pain me, I don't know what will happen. I went to the doctor the other day, and he gave me some tablets to take for the pain. Sometimes it helps, but sometimes I can still feel the pain.

"The Lord makes me forget all my troubles"

I get my day off on Sunday and Wednesday afternoon. Wednesdays I stay in the house, because sometimes I don't even know where to go in this city. I visit my church sisters sometimes. On Sunday, I go to church all day. I go at nine o'clock in the morning until twelve, then I go back again at three until ten-thirty at nights. To tell you the truth I feel happy there. When I am there the Lord makes me forget all my troubles, and the church sisters and brothers are good people, so we pray together and ask the Lord to make my paper come through.

Is the children I worry about most. Every day and night I ask the almighty God to watch over them for me, especially the three boys, you know how boy children are, they can get into trouble so easy, always in gangs and bad company. The girls I don't worry about so much, because they all join Bible class and keeping themselves good. My elder daughter, who is in the church, look after them, and I send home money every month for them. Right now, I get $300.00 a month, and I try and send home $200.00 for my family.

It hard on me, because I try to save a little money here too, so that when Immigration call me in, I will have money to show them, because a church sister told me that they look to see if you have lots of money in the bank, to see if you can support yourself or if you will be a burden on the government.

The Lord is my witness, I don't want to be no burden on this here government. I am a God-fearing woman and I want to work for my living.

Irma

> I remember I use to tell my mother that I wanted to be a teacher when
> I grow up.... She use to always tell me that if I study my books hard
> and pass my exams then I could make it in the world and be a teacher.

As a young girl growing up in rural Jamaica, Irma wanted to be a teacher someday. She loved books and remembers well her joy and enthusiasm when she played school with her playmates.

Irma also got a lot of encouragement from her mother. "Things was hard for her, she had to look after eight children alone, but she always encouraged us to do things." During Irma's childhood her mother supported the family by washing and cleaning other people's clothes and houses. Irma says that it was seeing how hard her mother had it that prompted her to strive to someday become a teacher.

When Irma failed her common entrance exams, however, she had to give up her plans for more education. It was an extremely painful time for her. She even lost speech for a while. Unable to go on with her schooling, she worked first as a higgler's helper (assistant to a market vender), and later as a dishwasher in Kingston. Irma talks about her four children, her relationship with her boyfriend and her job as a domestic worker in Canada.

Irma's disappointment in and doubts about the justice of the present way our society is organised filter through. "Now the way things is, I scared to make plans. Is like there is always disappointment." Nonetheless, she knows she is a survivor, "But I still have my dream to be teacher, I want to stay here and work for a few more years and then I'm going home to set up a school."

GROWING UP

"If I have a aim in view, I don't care who think I am foolish"

When I was growing up as a young girl I wanted to be a teacher. I use to admire my teacher, it was like she could read every book and spell every word. That is how I wanted to be. I remember that I use to gather up all the children in the yard every evening to play school. I would play teacher all evening until they all get tired and run off and leave me, or until their mother called them to wash the dishes or take care of a younger brother or sister. I remember I use to tell my mother that I wanted to be a teacher when I grow up. Things was hard with her, because she had to look after eight children alone, but she always encouraged us to do things. She use to always tell me that if I study my books hard and pass my exams then I could make it in the world and be a teacher.

Things was hard with my mother, very hard, for she use to clean people's houses and wash their clothes so that we could have a little money. My ambition was to get a good education and be a teacher and look after her. My sisters use to laugh after me and call me bookworm for I was always studying, but I didn't care what they call me, because that's how I am even now, if I have a aim in view, I don't care who think I am foolish. I use to study hard, I never really got involved in girlfriend and boyfriend business like my other sisters.

"It was like somebody throw a rockstone"

Well, it was coming near to common entrance exam. I study hard for the exam, but when the results came out I didn't pass. It was like somebody throw a big rockstone and hit me. I didn't talk to anybody for weeks, for I was sure I was going to pass that exam, so I could go to high school. For weeks I didn't talk, they even begin to feel that I had gone dumb. It was when they threaten to take me to Bellevue,[1] that I start to talk again. Well, as it so happen, I had to stop going to school, because my mother didn't have any money to pay for my lessons. So it was when I was twelve years old that my ambition to be a teacher died.

After I stop going to school, I help my mother in the house with the younger children, cooking and cleaning up until she came home from work. I remember sometimes, she would come home late at nights and tired. We girls use to help her soak her feet in a bucket of water to soak her corn. She had to walk five miles a day back and forth to go to work. If she was lucky, sometimes she would get a ride to work, if somebody who had a car was going in that direction, or else she walked.

"That was no life for a young girl"

When I got to fifteen years old, I got a job in the market. It was one of my mother's best friend. She is a higgler. We grew up in the country, a place call Highgate, in St. Mary. I use to help her carry the food to the market and help her set up the stall. But mostly what I did was watch so that nobody steal the food. When she go to the toilet, or to stretch her foot I would sell for her, but mostly I watch. But you know, as time goes by I started to get restless. For that was no life for a young girl. And all my friends were going to town to live. They use to come home on holidays with all sort of pretty things, and things look as if they were rosier in town. I bother and bother my mother until she decide to help me to go to town.

I was seventeen years old when I go to town. I didn't know anybody. I had a address with me that my mother gave to me to go and see a lady that she knowed. Everything seemed so different when I got off the bus. People running up and down, the bus, the cars, everything look bigger and faster than in St. Mary. I follow the directions that was on the paper until I got to the lady house. She wasn't really that pleased to see me. When she write mama in the country, she said she was doing good in town, but when I reached her house, things look like it was bad for her.

It turn out that she was staying with another friend who had four children, plus her three children in a little room in a tenement yard,[2] so you can see why she wasn't too happy to see me. But she didn't turn me out, though, and that night and for the next two weeks I slept with three of the older children on newspaper and a torn up sheet on the concrete floor. It was rough for me, because even though we were poor in the country, we always had food on the table and here in town, things were different. Some evening is turn cornmeal and water[3] we eat for dinner.

Eventually I found a job through another girl in a restaurant washing dishes. I couldn't thank her enough. Things couldn't get any rougher. In those two weeks that I was staying with my mother friend, I didn't sleep good. For it isn't easy sleeping on concrete with turn cornmeal in your stomach. They start me off at $15.00 a week. It wasn't much, but it was money, and I could get my meals free. Eventually I manage to find a room down the street from my mother friend and I shared it with two other girls. During that time, things were working out. I wasn't rich or anything. But life didn't seem hopeless. I was getting my meals free. And the rent wasn't that high, as I was sharing it with the two other girls. Plus, I had a boyfriend who was nice to me. So I could manage well, and even manage to send a little money home for mama. I became pregnant for my boyfriend and after the baby was born we started to live together in the same yard, but a different room. I still kept my job at the restaurant, and my boyfriend was working as a mechanic with his uncle.

I stayed in my job for five years and then I get moved up to cook. That was a lucky break for me, for by then I had two other children, so it was more mouth to feed. I got to really like the job. When I first move up to cook, I didn't like it too much, because it was so hot near the fire and at the time I was carrying my third baby and I was seven months pregnant. But after I had the baby, I got to like it.

"I was supporting the four children on $25.00 a week"

After the third baby, things started to go bad with me and my boyfriend. Sometimes he would sleep out, and I would hear from other people that he had girls. I wasn't getting any help from him at all with the children. He spent all his money drinking and gambling. When I threatened to leave him, he would beat me up. So then life was beginning to get unhappy for me. I got pregnant for him again, and there was nothing I could do. I was scared to move because I know he would just find me and beat me up more. Things was rough, because I was supporting the four children on my little pay, which by then was around $25.00 a week. I found that I had to take in people's clothes to wash so that I could make a little extra money. Once in a blue moon, if he was drunk and the children ask him for money to buy school shoes, he would give them. One evening I was home after work, and he came into the room and said to me, "Irma, I don't want you no more, I find a educated girl, she is pregnant for me, and we going to get married." I remember it clear, clear. That was the second time in my life that I felt as if a big rockstone had hit me and knock me out cold. I didn't answer him. I remember he grab me and shake me and shout at me to say something but I didn't. He sucked his teeth, pack up what clothes he had left in the room and just walk out on me and his four children. I didn't have to tell the children nothing, is as if they knew for they didn't ask me anything.

I couldn't manage alone with four children. So I sent the two youngest ones back to the country to stay with my mother. Things were still hard for me with the two older ones. But the good thing is that they are girls, so after school, they found work doing ironing and washing. I wasn't pleased with that. But there was nothing I could do, for we couldn't manage no other way. Eventually I had to send the two girls back to the country, too. Things was just too hard for me with them, and, you know, I use to get worried about them staying alone all the time when I was working late. I just worry all the time about them. I didn't want them end up pregnant.

"They asked me if I live in a tree in Jamaica"

In 1980 I came up on the work permit. I was very happy about coming up, because you hear from people all the time about how much money you can make up here and how good the opportunity is to uplift yourself. When I was coming up, two car-loads of friends took me to the airport. I promise to write everybody. I promise them that I would mail them a piece of the snow. On the plane I was looking forward to meeting my employers and the two children. It was like I was dreaming the whole time I was on the plane, about what Canada look like and the two children I was to take care of. Things didn't work out that way, though.

I didn't get to meet the children until the next morning because when I came Tuesday night, they were asleep. They gave me a room in the basement, and I had to use the bathroom upstairs. Well, the next morning

I woke early, at 5:30, and got dressed. I was a bit nervous about starting, for I didn't know what exactly was my duty. I sat and wait until 7:00. The missis call me out in the kitchen and gave me a list of things to do. Imagine, I just come off the plane, and she want me to wash windows. I told her that I didn't know how to wash windows from outside, and she told me that there was a ladder in the garage that I was to use. Then she lead me back in the basement and show me how to use the washer an dryer, and hand me three garbage bag full of clothes to wash and dry and iron. She told me she and her husband had to hurry off to work and that in the evening she would instruct me as to what my duties was to be. She just left like that. I was scared. I didn't know anything about Canada. As they leave that morning, the children woke up and one start laughing at me, making jungle sound. Asking me if I live in a tree in Jamaica. The children were nine and ten years old. After the children left for school I just wanted to pack my things and leave. But I remember how hard it was for me to survive and that was what make me decide to stay. And then again, I promise my older girl to put her through secretarial school.

My first day in Canada I will never forget. I try to climb on the ladder to do the windows, but I was so scared that I would fall that I didn't do it. So the whole day, I wash the clothes, dry them and begin to iron. That same day, I get my first cussing from the lady. She ask me why I didn't do the windows and when I tell her that I was scared, her remarks was that I was acting as if I don't know how to climb, she ask me if I didn't use to climb trees in Jamaica. I say yes and she said that it was the same way I would have to do to clean the windows. She inspect all the washing. That evening I was still ironing at 10:00 p.m., for she said she wanted me to finish up the ironing for the next morning I would have other things to do.

"On my days off she sends me to wash her friend's clothes"

That first week she really got her money worth out of me. The next day, she told me I had to cook the dinner and also clean the house. The children had no manners to me. They use to call me Blackie all the time and laugh. When I complain to her, she ask me if I wasn't Black. But it's not that you know, it's not that I is not Black, but I know that they was making fun of me. I stick out the job for one year and a half. And even when I make up my mind to leave it, I felt that Immigration might deport me, but it was just a chance I had to take. That woman was driving me like a slave. Is a lot of times when I was suppose to be on my days off that she would send me over to her friend house to wash clothes for them. When I complain she would ask me if is me washing them or the washing machine. I never use to get any extra money for that. So I was getting $494.00 every month. We really suppose to get

$710.00 a month. But out of that, $216.00 go for room and board. I don't even know why the government allow them to take $216.00 for room and board. Because when I was with her, God bless what food I eat that belongs to them. When I got to know the place a bit, I had to take money out of my own and buy food for me to eat. For is pure foolishness they eat. I love to eat rice and they hardly cook that. The little things they eat can't full my belly. When I just come here, I was always hungry in the night time. Is when I start to move around and know West Indian shops I start to eat good, so that money she take for food she shouldn't.

"Immigration doesn't want me to leave the job"

Well, it comes a time when I couldn't take it any longer. A girl I use to know in Jamaica and who was up here now told me about another lady who was looking for a girl. I went to see her and she hired me right away. I didn't tell her I was working for somebody, because I didn't want her to call up the lady. I got the job and that gave me enough time to go to Immigration and tell the lady that I was leaving.

The Immigration officer I saw wasn't happy when I told him I wants to leave the job. When I told him the reasons, he said that he was sure I could work it out with the lady. I wasn't sure what he would do to me, because he kept asking me about Jamaica and my children. I beg and plead with him and ask him to give me one more chance. I told him that I found a new job. I told him I was sure I was going to get on with the people. He sit across from me and look at me and tap his pen on the table for a long time. Then he said, "I will give you a chance, but I don't want to see you here again." I thank him, then I go home and pack up my things. I told her that I was leaving in two weeks time and she told me to leave now. I didn't ask no questions, I just pick up my suitcase and leave. I stay with a friend for two weeks until my next job start. I was nervous and scared. Because if Immigration found out that I did leave my first employer's house and not working in somebody else house they could deport me. I kept my fingers cross the two weeks. But they didn't find out.

"I get $350.00 a month, for the lady say I am on a year's probation"

The job I at now is better. I look after three children for a lady and her husband. The children have manners to me. They don't call me any names and I don't clean anybody house other than my employer. Still, because I live-in, it cause problems with my days off. For even on my days off I end up working. On this job I am not getting what Manpower say we should get. I get $350.00 a month because the lady say they want to see how I work out first. She say I am on a year probation, then if I pass, I will get the regular amount. I never hear of this law yet, but maybe it pass by Immigration and they didn't tell us.

"He started to feel me up"

The only problem I really had was with her husband brother. He visit them often, and any time he come, he would always be finding excuse to come into the kitchen, or come down in the basement where my room is. He always ask me about boyfriends. First I use to laugh and joke with him, you know, because I didn't want to go on like I am rude. But then it gets to a point where he ask me if I don't miss sex, if I have any since I come to Canada. I was nervous, for I don't know what to do. I didn't want to make any trouble for no one. So what I did was when I hear him coming, I would go to my room and lock up. Sometimes the lady would want me to do something in the kitchen. I think her husband knowed about his brother, because one time I was in the kitchen and his brother come in and sit down and start keeping up argument with me. Like that he never went to sex with a Jamaican woman before and he want to know if all the islands girls sex the same way. Mr. Hart came and peek and when he see his brother in the kitchen alone with me, he tiptoe and go back in the living room. He thinks I didn't see that but I did.

It got to the point where I had to talk to somebody, for he start to feel me up right there in the kitchen. I didn't know what to do. I didn't want to create no scene. I knowed I couldn't complain to Immigration. One day nobody was home and he come to the house. He try to push me down on the sofa but I manage to push him off me. I was shouting at him, but he only laugh and say that if is the last thing he get is to sex me.

"One minute it seems like you can talk to them, the next minute you can't"

Now that is the thing that is bothering me about this job. For I don't interested in any man. I just interested in saving my money to help my children and to get this landed here. I don't know what to do. I know I not going back to Immigration to complain. For just the other day they deport a girl for changing her job two times in six months. I feels sorry for her. Only God knows what she was going through. I am thinking of telling the lady I work with. But I don't know what she will do. You know, they are so funny, one minute it seem like you can talk to them and the next minute you don't know if what you say they will take as insult; is hard to know. All I can do now, is push him off when he come to trouble me. But you know, the thing hurt me very much. For I don't want no sex from him. Sometimes I feel like just stabbing him with the kitchen knife. But I know that is trouble.

I hear about the Immigrant Women's Job Placement Centre from a friend. She says I should go down there and talk to somebody, she give me the lady name. So when I get my next day off I am going to go there and tell her. Maybe she can help me try tell the lady I work with. I don't want to leave the job. Because it not bad. But I don't want to sex with the man's brother.

"I still have my dream"

You know, it so funny about life, you can't even plan it out. It didn't work out that way. Sometimes life just makes you feel sad. Sometimes when I sit and think about my life and how my ambition to turn a teacher never really turn out. Now the way things is I scared to make plans. Is like there is always disappointment following you. Right now I am doing upgrading in maths and English. After I finish that I want to get my grade twelve and thirteen. I don't know how long that will take, but I still have my dream to be a teacher. I want to stay here and work for a few more years and then I'm going home to set up a school in St. Mary. My two ambitions is to work and save money and to get my grade thirteen.

I don't know what is going to happen to that, because I don't know what kind of course Immigration want you to take before you get your landed. That is why I want to go down and see the lady at the Immigrant Women's Job Placement Centre. But like I say, I can't plan, for life never work that way for me. I don't know if I want my children to come up here... it's so many problems....

Primrose

They don't care about you, all they care about is the work to be done.
They don't care if you are crawling on your knee as long
as their job is done.

Primrose is a thirty-five year old Jamaican woman who came to this
country eight years ago on a Temporary Employment Visa. She has five
children, the youngest is twelve years old. The last time she saw any of them
was in 1976 when she left them behind in the care of her mother.

Primrose is a small and slender woman who looks much younger than her
thirty-five years. Looking at her, it is hard to believe that she is a mother of
five children.

At the beginning of our first interview Primrose was shy, reserved and
hesitant to talk about her work in the homes of Canadians, but this passed
as we became comfortable with each other. She speaks articulately,
forcefully. She is angry, and that anger spills out as she criticises the
Jamaican government for not informing women who leave to take domestic
jobs, about working conditions here.

She also gives us an insight into the relations between domestic workers
and their female employers and the lack of respect with which women in
her line of work are treated.

Primrose's work history is unusual. This is her fifth job as a domestic
worker since 1976 and she counts herself lucky. She says that other women
on the work permit are often harassed, threatened with deportation and at
times deported for changing their jobs, or questioning the long hours they
work.

Her church is a place of refuge for Primrose and many women like her
who live isolated from each other and from their community. She says that
by playing religious tapes and talking with God, she keeps her sanity when
the pressures of being a domestic worker become too much.

This is Primrose's story:

WORKING IN CANADA

"We are the ones who clean up their mess"

When I first came to this country, I came with three intentions — to help
my kids, to go to school to better myself, and to go to work and save some
money. But now that I'm here, I find you can neither save money, go to
school or send for my kids.

Canadians have the feeling that we are coming here to rob them, to take away their jobs, yet we are the ones who clean up all their mess, pick up after them. We take the jobs that they wouldn't take, and yet they hate us so much.

Sometimes I sit down and I consider, and I say that our government (in Jamaica) are very slack too. I say this when I face all the problems that we live-in domestic workers have, if and when they — the employers — go to our country, they don't get the treatment like we do here. I tell myself that if God help me and I get through in this country, when I go back to JA (Jamaica), I'm going to go to RJR[1] and JBC[2] radio station and announce to all the people the true story of Canada and Canadians. I want to somehow get to the government of Jamaica to let them know they are slack, cause if they had done better we wouldn't be under this pressure.

When I came here in 1976 to work as a live-in domestic worker, I left my five children behind with my mother. I have four girls and one boy. My youngest child is now twelve years old. My oldest daughter is presently on her own and second eldest is now married, so the rest of the children stay with her and her husband.

"I didn't know what I was getting into"

My first job was looking after a family of six — four children and the husband and wife. It wasn't that pleasant because I really didn't know what I was getting into. The first problem was I didn't use to get my pay on time. I had to remind the lady week after week. At the time I was getting $50.00 a week and the $50.00 couldn't stretch too far.

She was a nice person, but she had some problem with her husband and I didn't know that. When I wasn't getting my pay on time, I would ask her and she would say I must ask him, but I hardly saw him, so I continued asking her for it. I told her that when I use to work in Jamaica I didn't have to keep asking for my salary, that when I worked I got it. After a while she stopped paying me by the month and pay me every week. Then it happen that one time she had to go away from home and I ended up working four weeks without pay. The day she come back to the house was on my day off. I was going out so I turn to her and said I would like my pay now because I didn't get paid for four weeks. She turn to me and said, "Why didn't you tell him that, I'm not a mind reader". I said, "But you are the one that always pay me. When you go away you didn't say anything to me about how I would get my pay". Her remark at that was how did she know that Mr. So-and-So didn't pay me. Anyway, she gave me one week's pay. That got me a bit upset because I had worked for four weeks and now I was getting only one week's pay. Plus I was also a bit upset because she is responsible for paying me, because from when I was there I never had to go to the husband for my pay.

"I want to get what I work for and get it on time"

Right after I get my one week's pay I left and went down to Immigration. I explain to them what happen and they ask me if I want to leave. I say no, I just want to clear up about my salary so I can get what I work for and get it on time. One of the women down at the Immigration said I must go back to the house and ask her for the rest and hear what she say. The woman at Immigration said she would call me the following Monday to see what happened. She called me back the Monday and I told her that the woman I work for didn't respond. She said why didn't I leave and try to get another job. The next Sunday morning I leave a note explaining why I was leaving, I leave her key and I leave without my pay. I eventually got my pay because I went through Human Rights. It's after I leave that I found out that she was having problems with her husband, that he wasn't giving her the money for the house on time and that was the reason why I wasn't getting my pay on time.

The next job I had was with an elderly couple. The man was sick. The wife wasn't really sick, but she couldn't move around too well. I had to give him his bath, push him around in his wheelchair, take him to the washroom, feed him, get him dressed in the morning, undress him at night, fix up everything his wife choose for breakfast and lunch and supper. This job wasn't really bad — the couple were nice people.

But after a while the man pass away and she couldn't keep me any longer. She recommended me to a friend of hers not far from where I was with her. So I move from her to my third job.

This was with another family that included the husband, wife, a daughter and a son. The son was grown up, so he was in and out. I didn't really have a lot to do with him. I use to cook and wash for the mother, father and daughter and do the housework. The work wasn't that hard, and the woman was understanding and pleasant. We sat and talked a lot.

I started work at nine in the morning and work until about four in the afternoon. Most of my work was centred around the husband because he was sick. After a while he started to get sicker and had to go to the hospital and then from the hospital to the nursing home. He's still there. They couldn't afford to keep me after he went to the nursing home because the wife was strong and could do whatever there was to do around the house. After that job I went back down to Manpower and they gave me time to find another job.

Eventually I found my fourth job. I use to work with this man and his wife.

He could move around and look after himself, but she was a bit helpless, so I had to give her a bath, comb her hair, dress her, take care of the home, fix the meals and so on.

"They say I'm not entitled to a day off"

I really had a lot of problem with my days off. My days off was suppose to be Thursdays and Sundays. Sometimes I would leave Wednesday night after the lady was in bed and everything was o.k., because I'm really suppose to stop working at six. But I always have to make sure the lady is in bed and everything is O.K., so I usually left the house around nine or ten.

One Wednesday night I left around nine to be with some friends. The Thursday morning — my day off — I call the house just as a courtesy to find out how the lady is out how the lady is. Well, her husband's remark was "How do you expect her to be if you leave her?!" I said to him it's my day off, and he said to me that I had just started to work two weeks ago and I was not entitled to a day off. He was really rude to me, and then he hung up on me. I was a bit angry because he didn't have to talk to me like that, and he didn't employ me — it was the lady's daughter who employ me.

When I went back after my day off — the Thursday night — he told me that his daughter wanted me to call her. I called her, and she said she would be coming in the following day because she wanted to talk to me. I told her I had a few things I wanted to talk about too. She came in the morning, and before I could say anything she started shouting that she got me to take care of her mother and that I take off and leave her alone. I say to her it's my day off. She turned and said that I'm not entitled to a day off. I tell her that our arrangement was that I would get Thursday and Sunday off. I am entitled to it. But she didn't listen to me, she just went on and on and on. I eventually left that job because I just couldn't put up with it. It was like I was working all seven days a week.

"I don't want any more problems with Immigration"

After I left that job I had a hard time trying to get another one. It took me about four weeks and during those four weeks I had to go down to Immigration, carry names and places that I went for interviews all the time. Eventually I pick up this job that I am still in now. This job that I am in is my longest job in Canada and it is my worst job too.

I been working with this family soon four years now. I saw the job in the newspaper. When I went for the interview I didn't want to tell her that I was on the work permit. I was scared because there was a lot of people coming on the interview, and she might hire someone who was landed. But I didn't give up hope, I just sat and waited. After the interview I got the job.

I didn't say anything about the work permit for about a week. When I feel that I had fit in my position I told her I am on the work permit and I was just trying hard to get a job and I didn't want to lose this one, so that if she still consider me suitable I would be very happy. She said she would talk to her husband, and the following morning that I go in she told me she will do it.

This was around 1979. I started off getting $75.00 a week. Then they raise it to $100.00 a week, but I end up with about $90.00 and some change after taking out tax and other things. Now I'm getting $140.00 a week, but I take home $128.00. It's hard. It's really hard because I work long hours and I have to send home money for my children and mother.

The reason I stay in this job so long is because I don't want any more problem with Immigration. They gave me a lot of hassle when I change from the last few jobs I had, even after I tell them about the problems. One year ago they said they wanted to hold my passport, and that they are thinking of sending me back home because I seem to be having a lot of problems coping. So I stay in this one because I don't want to go through that again. Not that I am happy in this one.

"She don't matter who she crashes as long as she reaches"

The man is O.K., the kids are O.K. — one is three and one eight years old. But the wife is very domineering. She use to work out, but now she stops, so she's home every day. She about the same age as me, she thirty-eight years old. She's the type of person who if she want to go down the street, she don't matter who she crashes as long as she reaches. And if she want that done, you must do it right away — it don't matter what you are doing, no question ask.

I remember I went to the States with them for their vacation. I was in Sun Valley, there wasn't any Blacks anywhere around there, nobody I could really talk to. They went skiing, but I went with them to take care of the kids. It was very lonely. I had to stay and look after the little girl in the daytime because the little boy went skiing with them. If they come in, in the evenings and want to go out, then I would stay in and look after the two children. It was very cold most of the time. I didn't have anyone to talk to — during that whole time — because everyone was skiing.

One day when she came home from the skiing I told her how I was feeling. Her remarks was if I want somebody to talk to, go over to the station, there is a Black person over there. I say to her I didn't come here to look man, I come here to work. Before that on another occasion she told me that I must remember that I come there with them to work, so I just sort of reminded her.

"I was really hungry most of the time"

Then I told her about food, that I was hungry a lot of nights. She turned to me and said that there is no way she can cook my kind of food. I was really hungry most of the time, because their food is one little piece of potato, a little piece of carrot.

Another time I told her that I was feeling lonely so I wanted to go down to Sears to look around and buy something. She said it was fine, but I must take the baby with me in the stroller and go and pick up this box. There was no way I could manage because there was nowhere in the stroller that I can put this box. During those three weeks there I didn't even get one day off.

When we were about to come back to Canada she said I must go and pack up the children suitcase and also her suitcase. I didn't pack her suitcase because I knew that wasn't my job and she had a lot of time to pack her suitcase. The night she came in, she packed her suitcase and I packed the kids.

The morning we were leaving, she get up and fix breakfast, and I start to tidy up the place because of course I didn't want to leave the place dirty. When I went in the kitchen to have my breakfast, they had already had theirs, and I didn't see anything for me. No egg, nothing. Just dry bread, so I didn't have nothing more than just some tea.

When we were travelling now, they stop at some restaurant to get something to eat. She gave me the baby and a diaper and ask me to go into the restaurant toilet and change the baby. When I come back I went into the restaurant to join them. I pick up the menu sheet and I order a hamburger and some french fries. She turn to me and said why I ordering so much food and we going to have supper in a few minutes from now? Her husband turn to her and said we have over three, four hours left to travel before dinner. I felt so embarrass. Here I was standing and they arguing over me. I feel really embarrass and I wanted to pay for it out of my own money. But then I didn't know whether I would embarrass anyone if I did that. I didn't want to embarrass anyone the way they embarrass me because that is not my life style. So I just order some french fries, and sit quiet.

"As long as I live I will never go out with them again"

It was a really long trip — we had to travel for another four hours, stay in a hotel the night, and then take the plane back to Canada the following morning. When we reach the hotel, I put the kids to bed, and she said to me that she and her husband have to go back out, and what I want to eat. I say "whatsoever," and I waited, I waited, I waited, I waited, and they didn't turn up until three and a half hours later. In the meantime, I was hungry. I went downstairs the hotel and get a pop and a pack of biscuit. When they come back they brought a little something for me which looked like leftovers, so I told them that I wasn't hungry. Imagine, the whole day I went without food they went out and had their supper and then came back with something cold for me. Gas was killing me; even though I was hungry I couldn't eat it.

The next morning when we were going to take the plane back, she and her husband sit side by side, I believed that her husband and she would sit separate and both of them would sit with the kids. But that didn't happen. I sit with the kids. When we got off the plane I just kept walking out, I was so vex, but she just push the baby in my arms with the stroller, plus I had some other bags in my hands with my things. I will never forget that, and all she had was a little carrying bag. She just walk off and leave me because she was mad — I don't even know what at. I take my time and push and push the stroller with my bags, and then I reach inside the airport. When I reach the airport she start to fuss with me. I tell myself then and there that as long as I live, I would never go out with them again.

"In four weeks I didn't get a day off"

When I get back now — remember I was with them for four weeks, I didn't get one day off — I wasn't feeling well. There's this guy who use to pick me up every morning at my house because he drive in that direction. When he come to pick me up that morning I was sick and he said to me, "How you sick like that and you going to work?" I said to him I have to go, and he said, "You can't go to work like that." So I pick up the phone and dial the number, but I had to go to the washroom because I was beginning to vomit. I gave him the phone and tell him when she answers, "Just tell her for me that I am sick and I can't make it today." When I come back he told me that she was mad and that she said I must call her. When I call her and explain to her that I had a upset stomach, she was very nasty to me, and then she slam the phone down in my ears. Even the next morning I still felt sick, but I got dressed and went to work.

When I went to work I realise that the same day when I called in sick, she went ahead and put ads in the paper, because people kept calling about my job. I took their names and phone numbers, and when she come home that day, I give them to her. The evening when I give her the phone numbers, she turn to me and shout, "Imagine! I have to go to work, and when I ready to go to work, you are calling me to tell me that you are sick and can't come in!" She went on and on, very nasty. I don't even remember some of the things she said to me — I just stood there and listened to her because there was nothing I could do. I know she is a problem and I can't get on with her, but I also know that Immigration is another problem. So what can I do?

"She's a hassle, but Immigration is also a hassle"

It was really bad after that because the little boy started mimicking his mother. I try to live it down until her husband come one day to talk to me and I say to him, "A few weeks ago on the vacation — while I was there I had something to say, but I try to keep it in because I didn't want to spoil your vacation. The way in which your wife talk to me through the whole vacation, I wasn't happy." He just became angry and said I was pointing my finger at him and that I mustn't point at him. So then I just stop talking because I realise that it wasn't making any sense.

I don't know when it will end. I'm still with them even now, with a lot of heartache.

Right now I'm suppose to work from ten in the morning until six in the evening — that was what we agreed upon. Now she told me to come at eight in the morning, and sometimes I stay until seven-thirty or eight in the evening, especially if she is going shopping or want to go do her hair. She don't even call to tell me that she will be late; she just comes in at whatever time, and I am not suppose to say anything.

She don't want me to question anything or talk back. At the same time she can't tell her eight year old child to go take up that without he asking why — but they want to tell you and you have to do it. It hurt me every morning to go there. Some of my friends say if I am not happy, why don't I just leave. I can't leave. She is a hassle, but Immigration is also a hassle, and you never know when they might decide to send you home.

They know we are overworked. I have a girlfriend and every time she has to go down to Immigration she say, "I'm going for sentence now. Down big yard." So if I'm going tomorrow, I'll say, "I'm going for sentence," and they'll say, "Good luck!" because any time you going down there is problems. If the government wanted to do something about it, they could. We have to live in the employer's house and they are collecting so much money for room and board.

I know the government could arrange somewhere for the people like us to stay. What the employers are claiming for and not spending, the government would have that money to spend to help the country. They say they are feeding you — God bless what you are getting, a piece of toast.

"This is the worst life I ever come across"

I sit and think, and I say this is the worst life I ever come across. The worst. Sometimes I ask myself how I really leave my job back home and come here. My girlfriend, she didn't have any friends here and we use to work close home. Where she was working there wasn't any Black face around, no one for her to talk to. Then this woman, her employer, wanted somebody and she write and tell me and I come up. But if I really knew all the details and how I would be treated, I wouldn't be here. Back home I use to do nursing aid in a public hospital.

One morning I came into work a little late and she turned to me and said, "Imagine! I'm trying to avoid the kids and you are coming in at this hour!" I didn't say nothing; I just go and do my job. She is telling me the other day when I ask her if I could leave early, stop working at five o'clock, that Immigration this and that, always bringing up Immigration when I ask to get off a little early. So I turned to her and I say, "Immigration say I must work from ten until six and I am here every morning from eight." She turned to me and said to me, "Does Immigration know that you live out?" I said no and she smiled. Then she said to me, "Why don't you go in a factory and work?" She knows I can't do that — she know we can only do domestic work while we are on the work permit. She also know I'm not suppose to be living out. So she take those things and hold against me, so I keep quiet about the hours I'm suppose to work.

I'm telling you it's not pleasant. My employer stop working now, and she is home during the days, except if she goes out for a couple of hours sometimes. I do everything. I work hard because she can't do anything. She can't lift a straw because she say she's paying me to do all that. I wash, I clean, I cook because she can't cut nothing. She can't even wash her pantyhose. You have to do everything. Nowadays since she stopped working, she sit around all day, not doing nothing. At night time when she know her husband coming home, she run around like she doing this and she doing that. It's a big house, three floors. Even now, milk to buy and she can't go to buy it. I have to dress the little girl and take her with me even though she is in the house. Even now that she not working, I still have to do these things. The other day when I take the kids to school the teacher had to say, "But I don't even know the little girl's mother!"

"A lot of people try to get out of domestic work because of the conditions"

I think when people like us coming into this country they should have somebody to talk to them and let them know what to expect. Coming from your country and then getting into something like this, it can really shake you up. This is some of the things that cause a lot of divorce in Canada. If they had treat people that come to work on the permit like human beings and not as slaves, then a lot of people wouldn't end up marrying to the wrong person. A lot of people try to get out of domestic work because of the conditions.

We pay room and board and God bless what they give you to eat. And when income tax time come, the employer claim for so much. You have your kids back home and can't even find enough money to send home, and when you claim income tax, they are telling you that you are not entitled to that. At the same time, they are claiming what they are not entitled to. They are not spending and they are getting it.

We come working like slaves in this country, giving the government money, and we not getting back nothing because we have to pay pension, we have to pay insurance, we have to pay a lot of stuff. God know how I survive, but I do. Is only the mercy of God help us. If you check the churches in Canada, you see that ninety-five per cent of the church is on work permit. That's the only place they can go and get a peace of mind. It seems like it's not really worth it. I just here because I give up so much to come here. Many times I think of going back, but you keep saying next year will be better, next year will be better, and then it end up worse, and you stay here not achieving nothing. If you try to find things and you end up succeeding, then you can say you fight life and you achieve something out of it, and it makes you become stronger in life. But if I didn't have a family back home, maybe I wouldn't bother.

"I hang on, I have to"

Sometimes people say to me, "When you go to States with your employers why do you come back, why not just stay there?" But I believe in honesty and if I go there I will have to be hiding. I don't want to do that, so I may as well stay here and face it here until the time comes for me to get my landed, until the time when God feel that the time is right and when I can't stand it anymore, he will pull out the stumbling block. He going to do it, so I just hang on there. I bought myself some religious tapes and when things burn me, when things hurt me, I lock myself up in the washroom with the tapes and sing and pray and cry. I have to do that or I don't know where I would end up.

They don't care about you, all they care about is the work to be done. They don't care if you are crawling on your knees as long as their job is done. You are not suppose to be sick, you always suppose to be on top of it. I know old iron break down, but you suppose to be at all times strong and healthy to do their jobs. You suppose to be like a computer, at all times ready to do everything they say without any questions asked.

Gail

> I gave the woman around the desk my form... she look at it and then
> she called another woman who looked at it.... "Sorry this course is not
> for you. Immigration has told us to look out for these social insurance
> numbers beginning with number nine, and refuse all of you. You are
> not allowed to do these courses."

Gail is a bright and forthright Trinidadian woman in her mid-twenties.
She is very clear about her reasons for coming to Canada as a domestic
worker on a work permit. "Education," she says, prompted her to come, and
she came the only way she could, as a domestic worker.

Her experience in Canada is not unlike that of the other women in this
book. She too has put in long hours at low pay for employers who have only
their own needs in mind. But she has been luckier than most in the sense
that her present employer was once a domestic worker who came to
Canada as a nanny. Gail thinks that this has made her employer more
sensitive and respectful of her, and says this is the best job she has held in
Canada.

In this chapter Gail talks at length about problems she encountered while
trying to enroll in a basic computer program at night school.

This is Gail's story:

EDUCATION

"When you come here it's too late to back out"

I didn't just leave Trinidad because I wanted to come to Canada. I know
how cold Canada is so me ain't just want to come here for nothing. But
when you finish going to high school in Trinidad, if you didn't pass the
amount of subjects that you suppose to, and you don't have the money to
go to university, then you just have to do any little thing like work in a store,
clean house, wash clothes, anything. So education-wise, Canada is land of
gold for me, that the only reason I came here.

I came out here the only way I could. You see, it's really hard to get a
permit to Canada to come to school unless you have money, lots. So the
only other route for some of us who don't have lots of money is to take the
domestic approach. And when you come here, and start working and
realise what you really got yourself into, it's too late to back out. So you
know, it was the same with me, I started thinking, "What did I get myself
into?" and then I said to myself, "Best I go back home, but go back home,
how? to what?" My mother just borrow $1,000.00 to put me in a plane to

Canada. When you are coming up here on a work permit you have to buy a two-way ticket, so because of this you tend to stick it out, because the money is already spent.

These books like what you are doing need to be written, but they need to be sent down there in the Caribbean, so that before other women come up as domestics, they know what they getting themselves into. When you are down there, you tend to think that Canada is great, until you really come up and realise that what you really coming up to be is somebody's servant.

"I was treated to know your place"

I have been in Canada for over six years. And in that time I've worked with four employers. The first people I worked for were very nice to me. They had given me the basement, well-carpeted, my own T.V. and I was comfortable. When the day was over I use to go downstairs and lock my door, and I was in my own little place. The woman use to tell the children to leave me alone after a certain hour every day, not to go in my room. I had my weekends off, and I could use the back door to get out and come in and nobody would bother me.

The man was nice too, but still, I always feel very uncomfortable because the woman had this attitude that-you-are-here-to-be-a-servant. Let's face it. They are white elite and I is Black. So I was treated as know-your-place-you-are-here-to-do-this-and-that's-all-there-is-to-it. But it's hard to tell yourself, "I am only here to do this" — domestic work — when really I am living here twenty-four hours a day. I feel as if this is my home. It is my home, this is where I live. It's not like I come to work for them and then evening time I leave and go home. When you are living with them, they make you feel as if you really don't belong, and where the devil do you really belong? It's a funny thing to happen to us, because it make us feel like we don't know if we coming or going.

I don't know whether to say that they should really ban the whole goddamn thing of having people come up here and work as domestics, but something has to be done about the conditions, because this live-in thing really puts us in a funny situation.

My second job was with a single mother with three kids. The first people I was working with didn't really need me anymore after a time because the children had all reach school age and the mother decided to stay home. It was they who helped me to find the second job. Their neighbour had a sister who needed a sitter and they recommended me. Like I said, she was a single mother with three kids, and she was going through a divorce at the same time. My bedroom was right to the children's bedroom, and her bedroom was way off. The children were in my room twenty-four hours a day. Even if it was my day off, they were in my room and I still had to do things for them. If I wanted some peace and sanity, I had to get out of the house, and just go for long walks. Sometimes I would want to just stay in my room and lock the door, but how do you do that in somebody's home? If it's your day off, and something fall on the ground, you feel you have to wipe it up. Some night she wasn't coming home, and the husband would come all the time and cause problems. It was a terrible situation for a young person like me to be in, so I had to leave that job, I just wasn't comfortable there and most of the time I was scared about what would happen next. In that second job I was getting $120.00 a week.

"Our bosses ain't going to tell us about any laws to protect us"

Well, from that job, I went and work for the Scotts. They were nice, but they only thought of themselves. It's bad to say all Canadians are like that, but from my experience they tend to think that if you get your landed status you are going to leave them. They don't want you to progress at all, they want you to remain a babysitter all your life, and this was how the Scotts were.

I remember one time I went into Immigration to renew my permit to work and the Immigration officer ask me if I wanted to sign up and come in to see about my landed. I told her yes, and when I went home I told Mrs. Scott. She didn't want to give me any time off. She told me that she and the husband is working and I must wait for a little while longer. Well, eventually after a few months, she told me I could make the appointment. Well, I didn't get to go in to Immigration, because her mother died and she and the husband left for England, so I was left with three children to look after. I had to call Immigration and cancel the appointment. When she did come back, it was around time to renew my permit again, so when I went in, I made another appointment to go see about getting my landed, but I had to end up cancelling that one, too, because after her mother died and she came back from England she took it very badly and she was put in a mental home.

Her husband had his own business, so he was hardly home and I was looking after the three children from morning till they went to sleep. I know it was hard on him, but he could have made it possible for me to go in. In my situation I couldn't say anything. I just couldn't get up and say, "Well, I am going and if you want to fire me, fire me," because I know I would lose my job. People keep saying that it's easy to report your employer, that you can just go in to Immigration and report them. But it's not easy, and those people who keep saying it's easy, I want them to try it. I know I don't feel comfortable calling Immigration and telling them that my boss don't want to give me time off to go and see about my landed, it sounds funny. It was after they went back to England and I lost my job and found another one that I eventually went in and applied for my landed.

The people I work with now are very, very nice. This job I am doing is the best I've had since I have been in Canada. The woman understands the situation very, very much. She is from Scotland, she came here as a nanny a few years ago, then she met a lawyer and they got married. So she understands very much what it's like being a domestic worker. If she wants me to work overtime or on my time, she either pays me for it or she make it up in time. I also get my two weeks vacation with pay. She knows exactly what she went through and she hasn't forgotten, so it really is the best one when it comes to doing this kind of work. Right now I am living out on my own and I tell you it really make a difference as to how you feel about yourself.

It's so easy to feel restricted when you are a domestic worker. Everything you do, you have to let a Immigration officer know, if you leave the country they have to know, if you go to school they have to know — that is the part I don't like — and that is why I want to get my landed status. I want to be able to go to school free and without any complication. Every time I want to do a course I have to take time off from work and go in to Immigration. Every time I sign up for a course I have to take the form in to them for them to sign and say it's all right, then I have to wait, wait for them to give their permission. It's so stupid and it waste so much time. I think they should pass a law saying that all domestics could go to school instead of having to go in to them all the time to check before you do the course. Another thing with Immigration is that the laws that they does pass, they don't let us know what they doing. If I don't call somebody at a community agency and say, "So what's going on with Immigration these days," I wouldn't know. Probably our bosses do know, but they ain't going to tell us either, because they don't want us to know about any laws to protect us. Immigration should find a way to let us know what is going on so that we will know how to advance ourselves. But, they don't do that, they just treat us like stupid little Black people who come here to do only one kind of work.

"Immigration don't make any effort to get news to us"

I did not even know that they had passed the law saying that domestics could now go to school. I wasted a whole year not knowing. One day I called up my friend who work at a community agency and I said to her that I really want to go to school. She said to me that they have passed a law saying that you can go to school since last year. Well, I never knew that, and I do read, believe me, I do read. They (Immigration) don't make any effort to get information to us. The only other way, besides my friend, I find out anything is when I read these Black newspapers. Even after you find out these things and try to enroll in certain courses, you come up against problems.

"This course is not for you"

I was trying to get into a basic course in computers, in order to get into Ryerson Polytechnical school. To continue the computer course you have to start off with this basic course. I tried many times to get into the course but it was always filled. Well, this time I decided to go and try again at this secondary school that I heard was giving the course. I left work on my evening off to go and get signed up.

I was the fifth person in line when it was my turn to go up. I gave the woman around the desk my form that I filled out She look at it and then she called another woman, who looked at it, who called another man, he looked at it and they all looking at this piece of paper that I had signed for the course. Eventually the man said to me that I had to come with him and go and see somebody else, so I left with him and went to see another woman and she looked at it and said, "Sorry, this course is not for you." So I said, "What's the problem?" And she said, "It's your social insurance number. Immigration has told us to look out for these social insurance numbers beginning with the number nine,[1] and refuse all of you. You are not allowed to do these courses."

I told her that I found that strange because Immigration gave us domestics permission to go to school. She kept saying no, that Immigration had told them to look out for people with social insurance numbers starting with nine, and that we were not allowed to go to school. I ask her to keep the form and told her that I was going to Immigration to straighten it out, but she told me to take the form with me, she said that she couldn't keep it.

The following day, I called Immigration and they told me that she had made a mistake and that I should go back to the school and tell them this. So I called the school during the day when I was at work and I explained to the woman what had happened. She said that there was nothing she could do because my problem was with the night school, so I should contact them. By then I was so frustrated that I called my friend who is a community worker and I told her what had happened. She told me that she would call and try to find out some information and that I should go back to the school in the evening and explain what happened.

Well, I did go back in the evening, and, of course, when I got there the course was filled. I said to the woman at the desk, "Do you remember me? I came yesterday, you made an error." She cut me off and said that there was nothing she could do, that the course was filled.

I left the school, and the next day I called back again and try to explain to the woman again. I said, "I really think you should let me into the course, seeing that I was there yesterday and it wasn't my fault that it is filled up." She started shouting at me, "This course is not for you people and there is nothing I can do about it, Immigration told me to do this." So I said to her, "Immigration could not have told you to do that because I spoke to Immigration..." and she cut me off and say, "Well, if it wasn't Immigration it was the Ministry of Education, but somebody told me not to accept you people into these courses." I was angry, so I said, "What do you mean by 'you people'?" She didn't answer me, so I ask her again, but she only said, "There is nothing I can do for you, the course is filled, and you people are not allowed to do this course, I don't know who told me, but somebody told me that." Then she hanged up the phone in my ears.

I was ready to cry, I felt so angry and helpless. So I called my friend, the community worker, and told her what had happened. She called the school and told them she was working with a community agency and she related the situation to the person. The person she spoke to told her the reason why I was rejected was because I am not a landed immigrant and I couldn't take the course unless I paid to do it. My friend asked her if she had explained this to me yesterday, but the woman didn't answer her. She just said that the course was very expensive and that I wouldn't be able to pay for it, that it would cost me about $300.00. My friend told her that that wasn't the point, that if she had told me I have to pay for the course that I would have paid for it. After that my friend spoke to the principal of the school and told him that, quite frankly, it was not fair to me, especially the remark the woman made to me earlier. (That woman was the vice-principal.)

"She didn't know any better' is just a cover-up"

The principal told my friend that it was an error on the vice-principal's part, that she didn't know better. So my friend told the principal that something was going to be done about the whole situation. It was right then that the principal said it was an error on their part, and that my friend must tell me to come to the school right away and they would see if there is any room for me in the course. I reached the school around 7:00 p.m. and they had my papers all signed up and a place for me in the course. Today, I have my certificate saying that I have passed the course and I have not been charged a cent to do the course.

Even though I have my certificate, I still worry about the other women who will get turn away from that programme because they don t have anybody to help them speak up. This excuse that "she didn't know any better" is just a cover-up. I want to know where did she get that information from in the first place? I don't know and the principal just coolly covered it up.

"I know I'm going to go back home eventually"

After I get my landed I want to do two more courses, one a continuation of the computer course and also a course in the Montessori[2] school, because I want to open a Montessori school when I go back home. I don't really want to live here because I could never bring my son here. I know that. And I can't leave him in Trinidad forever, so I know I'm going to go back home eventually. It's just the schooling that I want here in Canada.

I have a son, but I've never told anybody, not even my employers, the Immigration or anybody. I just don't trust anybody that much, but I would really like to put it into my story because a lot of people back home don't know the consequences of that.

When I was in Trinidad and went to Immigration there, the guy said to me when he gave me the form to sign, "Do you have any kids?" and I said yes. He said that people who have children are not usually accepted to come to Canada, because a lot of employers up here will think that if you have a child back home you are going to miss the child, and you will either want the child to come up, or you might want to go back home soon to look after your child, and that they don't want to waste their time sponsoring somebody into the country and in three months time they get homesick for their children. He said it's best to say that you have no children. So I signed up and say I had none.

Now I have to live with that lie. I now realise I could never get my child to come here, because as far as Canada is concerned, I have no children. How could I come out now all of a sudden and say I have a son? I can't take the chance. I know people who they take away their landed from because of that same thing. It wasn't really my fault, I didn't know better at the time. The Immigration officer in Trinidad told me that whoever is sponsoring you doesn't like to know that you have a big tie in Trinidad if they know you have a tie back home, whether boyfriend or children, they won't sponsor you. I don't know when I will see my son again, but I hope it won't be much longer. It's hard to go home like this, without making any progress. You know, five, six years meet you here and you ain't getting nowhere, no further really, you still in the same thing. You think, "Well, maybe I should go back home," but then you say, "But God, how am I going to go back home now, it's six years and I am still the same way I came, so I'm gonna hold on," and you hold on, and you hold on, it's over six years I here, and I still holding on.

Shattering the Silence

You have just read the testimonies of ten West Indian working class women employed as domestic workers. For their voices to ring fully, they need to be heard over the clamour of their employers who, after all, have a vested interest in keeping them mute. Shattering this silence, winning good working conditions and pay, and dignity on the job for domestic workers will take the active support of many women and men.

Unlike most other workers, the majority of domestic workers are imported labour. They do not share a common workplace and Ontario law denies them the basic right to organise into a trade union to bargain with their employers in order to improve their wages and working conditions. They are not protected by the provisions of Ontario's health and safety legislation, nor are they covered by the province's workers' compensation law. In short, what most workers are fighting to maintain, or even improve, domestic workers have yet to gain.

In Ontario, as in other provinces, provincial law sets the minimum wage for most workers. And most, but not all, workers in Ontario have basic trade union rights. But, as the Ontario Federation of Labour noted in its 1982 Statement on Labour's Rights, neither the letter nor the spirit of the Ontario Labour Relations Act extends to domestic workers.[1]

Nor can domestic workers count very much on the basic and rather minimal protection of the province's Employment Standards Act, the law covering most non-unionised workers. To begin with, even though the minimum wage of $3.50 an hour (1983) is the lowest in the country, employers can legally pay domestic workers even less — $3.00 an hour.[2] As well, the parts of the law covering the hours of work, overtime pay and public holidays — rights even most non-unionised workers take for granted — do not even apply to domestic workers.[3] Instead, domestic workers are covered by a special regulation which, besides providing little protection, is difficult to enforce.

There are three reasons why the situation of domestic workers in this province has changed little over the past century. To begin with, most are immigrant women on work permits. Secondly, housework and who shall do it remains fixed in private life as a matter of individual responsibility. Thirdly, that housework remains an individual problem to be solved in individual homes makes it extremely difficult to cast a public eye on domestic workers' pay and working conditions, particularly since a domestic worker employed on a work permit who speaks out against her employer may very well find herself without a job and thus subject to deportation.

These final pages cannot exhaust these topics. There are, however, some basic questions which need to be raised on the nature of paid domestic work and on housework, questions that the mainstream women's movement has failed to take up, largely because of its white middle class bias. Nonetheless, what the women who spoke out in this book make clear is that domestic workers need full and complete labour rights. To those who would argue that the employers cannot afford the cost, it is enough to remind them that the same timid lament was raised about an end to child labour and about the demand for an eight hour day.

Few people today would dispute that housework is work, whether paid or unpaid. One women's organisation has even called for "wages for housework" as its main strategy for improving the lot of women.[4] Among the many things this slogan and the thinking behind it ignores, however, is that Black women have been receiving "wages for housework" for decades in payment for the housework they do for white women.[5]

And like their European sisters who worked as domestics at the turn of the century, Black domestic workers flee "wages for housework" at the earliest opportunity for other waged work, even at low pay and in poor working conditions. Canadian historian Wayne Roberts describes the situation of domestic workers at that time and quotes the lament of those whose service they fled:

> The democratic aspirations of working girls rebelled against the norms of service... as they deserted for a factory life of "monotonous toil and sordid degradation, relieved only by flirtation and dress" and rewarded by independence and freedom when work was done. Meanwhile, mistresses were exhausting every source of potentially cheap labour in a fruitless search to find replacements for their constantly fleeing employees. [6]

In recent times the source of this cheap labour has most often been women from the Caribbean and Asia, both areas of high unemployment. But I have yet to meet an immigrant domestic worker who would be willing to stay in this work if other jobs were available to her here or in her home country. Nor have I met anyone who aspired to a life of domestic work as a child or who dreamed that her daughter would some day take her post. On the contrary, the women whose stories appear in this book and the scores of other domestic workers I have talked with over the years are determined that their daughters will have work that is meaningful and less backbreaking.

In part, this search for other options springs from the long hours and the low pay. But this is not the only reason that employers are likely to continue to "find it so hard to get good help." The private organisation of housework also pushes domestic workers to seek other employment. Charlotte Perkins Gilman, writing at the beginning of this century, said it first and said it best:

> ... (T)he domestic system of feeding, clothing, and cleaning humanity
> costs more time, more strength, and more money that it could cost in
> any other way except absolute isolation. [7]

In short, domestic workers leave their jobs because they too want the alternatives to the "continuous effort (which) produces utter exhaustion"[8] that the women who employed them already have.

But this shared rejection of housework, paid or not, does not necessarily make for shared perceptions between domestic workers and their female employers. The lived relations between the woman-as-mistress and the woman-as-servant are complex and rarely mentioned even in contemporary writings on women and work. Even the feminist woman-as-mistress is usually silent on the topic in public. She may speak of having "solved the housework question" by employing domestic help, but she most often says nothing about the employer-employee relationship. It remains private, invisible, exempt from the feminist principle "the personal is political." It is when the woman-as-servant speaks that the relation begins to take shape:

> I could use the back door to get out and come in and nobody would
> bother me. Really there were nice people, but I always feel very
> uncomfortable, because the woman had this attitude that you-are-here-
> to-be-a-servant. Let's face it. They are white and elite and I is Black...
> So I was treated as know-your-place, you-are-here-to-do-this-and-that-
> is-all-there-is-to-it. [9]

In part, it is because housework takes place in private homes that helps to paper over mistress/servant relations. But it is also made invisible by an assumption that all too often goes unchallenged within the women's movement — the notion that all lived experience between women is reducible to the presence or absence of sisterhood. What gets forgotten in the struggle to make changes in our male-dominated society is that there are degrees of subordination and domination. The (usually) white female employers of Black and Asian domestic workers, although themselves members of a subordinate group because of their sex, are also members of the dominant group by virtue of their race and class, and quite "normally" share the assumptions on race and class held by their (usually) white male counterparts.

> Even though most of us do not like to think of ourselves as either
> believing in, or engaging in... domination, it is, in fact, difficult for a
> member of a dominant group to do otherwise. But to keep on doing
> these things, one need only behave "normally." [10]

So long as domestic work continues to be a private responsibility — in keeping with the beliefs of the dominant group on how such work should be organised — the situation of the women interviewed and others like them will continue to be marked by exploitation. No amount of sisterhood can erase the line between woman-as-mistress and woman-as-servant. Yet there are alternatives to leaving housework and thus paid domestic work as an individual problem to be solved as income and preference allow. Taking housework out of the private and into the public realm, looking at it like a public utility, was first proposed by Charlotte Perkins Gilman over eighty years ago. She advised that we "... put these poor antiquated 'domestic industries' into the archives of past history and let efficient modern industries take their place, doing far more work, far better work, far cheaper work in their stead."[11] And, in the words of a contemporary writer,

> ... (H)ousework need no longer be considered necessarily and unalterably private in character. Teams of trained and well-paid workers' moving from dwelling to dwelling, engineering technologically advanced cleaning machinery could swiftly and efficiently accomplish what the present-day housework (and domestic work) does so arduously and primitively.[12]

Bringing housework and its poor sister, paid domestic work, out of the private and into the public promises to be a long struggle. After all, "socialised housework implies large government subsidies in order to guarantee accessibility to the working-class families whose need for such services is most obvious."[13]

In the meantime, women who work as domestics, whether here on work permits, "landed," or native-born, need the same labour rights as other workers, especially the right to join the labour union of their choice and to bargain collectively for better wages and working conditions.

How do we organise to change the law to give domestic workers the same protection as other workers? What about the practical difficulties of organising? After all, it has been argued, domestic workers face their employers individually in private homes where they have little privacy after a long work day. And what about the fear of deportation for those whose work permits tie them to a specific employer? Is there really any reason to think these women will take steps on their own behalf? The task is not impossible, since there are historical and contemporary precedents both in Canada and in the United States. In the United States, a country where both the letter and spirit of the legislation governing unionising campaigns is heavily weighted in favour of the employer, but where domestic workers do have the right to form unions, they are unionising. In California, the scene of many bitter labour struggles, the United Domestic Workers of America has nearly 400 private housekeepers under union contract as well as representing 3,500 domestic workers who are employed by firms that provide homemaker services to the disabled, etc. If current unionising drives are successful the UDW will triple its membership by the end of 1983.

Throughout the history of the recruitment of Caribbean women for domestic work in Canada, there has been a tradition of informal self-organising and of support from within the Black community, particularly in Toronto.

The first Toronto group to take up the situation of domestic workers was the Negro Citizenship Association (NCA), which set up a hostel and meeting place for these workers in the mid-1950's. Domestic workers used the hostel on their days off to meet other women like themselves, to get information on how to get on in the city, to exchange jokes, and to cook the food they were forbidden to cook in the homes of their employers. The NCA also held dances for its members. This organisation operated until the early 1960's.

The Universal African Improvement Association has long been a place where domestic workers go for help, information and a space to meet among themselves. The Jamaican Canadian Association has, since its inception in the early 1960's, also taken an active role in providing support to domestic workers. As well, during the 1970's members of the Black Education Project acted as advocates for domestic workers in pay disputes and other matters.

The Domestic Workers Group (now known as Domestic Workers United), organised in the early 1980's, acts as an advocate in disputes with employers or in problems with Immigration, provides information on topics ranging from training courses to how to file an income tax return, and organises social events. Labour Rights for Domestic Servants, a multi-racial group organised around the same time as the Domestic Workers Group, carried out similar activities but has had more resources. Utilising the services of a free legal counsel, Labour Rights for Domestic Servants has successfully pressed claims for back wages under the Ontario Employment Standards Act, including a claim against Ontario government minister Larry Grossman. Community agencies such as Immigrant Women's Job Placement and the Immigrant Women's Centre are also places domestic workers turn to for help.

What domestic workers lack, however, are sufficient means to enforce their rights as workers. In particular, active support of a public determined to put an end to this exploitation of women and of labour.

There are several things the reader can do to help domestic workers win full trade union rights. Here are a few:

Get in touch with one of the organisations listed at the end of this book.

Pass a resolution in your local union and in your municipal and provincial labour organisations calling for full trade union rights for domestic workers.

Raise the issue in your riding association and pressure your MPP to put forward legislation to amend Ontario labour laws to include union rights for domestic workers.

Organise petition campaigns demanding union rights for domestic workers.

Pressure the federal government to provide protection for domestic workers on work permits who lose their jobs, and thus risk deportation, because of disputes with their employers.

Make union rights for domestic workers an issue in your women's groups. Raise it as an important issue at International Women's Day activities.

The issues raised in this book cannot be exhausted here.

I would be sorely remiss, however, if I failed to pay tribute to a domestic worker whose name may go unrecognised but whose action long ago still brings me courage. Her name was Rosa Parks. She was a Black maid in Montgomery, Alabama. It was December 1955. Bone-tired from a long day of scrubbing and sweeping, washing and ironing, cooking and cleaning, she wanted only to sit. "No," she said, when told to give up her white-only seat on a city bus and move to the back where it was standing-only. "No." The next day a Black community organisation, the Montgomery Improvement Association, began what was to have been a one-day bus boycott in support of Rosa Parks. This boycott lasted another 380 days. By the time it was won, the modern Civil Rights Movement had spread throughout the Southern United States.

Organisations

INTERCEDE
Toronto Organisation for Domestic Workers' Rights
489 College Street
Suite 402
Toronto, Ontario
M6G 1A5
(416)324-8751

Immigrant Women's Job Placement Centre
546A St. Clair Avenue West
Toronto, Ontario
M6C 1A5
(416)656-8933

Women Working with Immigrant Women (WWIW)
307 Wyandotte Street East
Windsor, Ontario
N9A 3H7
(519)973-5588

Ottawa-Carlton Immigrant Services (OCISO)
18 Louisa Street
3rd Floor
Ottawa, Ontario
K1R 6y6
(613)238-4256

Household Workers' Association
5309 Brebeuf
Montreal, Quebec
H3J 3L8
(514)525-6859

Alberta Network of Immigrant Women
233 10th Street North West
Calgary, Alberta
T2N 1V5
(403)270-7670

Household Worker Support Centre Association of Alberta
#2 - 8915-99 Street
Edmonton, Alberta
T6E 3V5
(403)439-5269

Immigrant Women's Association of Manitoba
Rm. 307, 323 Portage
Winnipeg, Manitoba
R3B 2C1
(204)943-8612

Women Working with Immigrant Women (WWIW)
100 Charing Crescent
Fredericton, New Brunswick
E3B 4R7
(506)454-1821

National Organisation of Immigrant and Visible Minority Women
(NOIVMWC)
100 Charing Crescent
Fredericton, New Brunswick
E3B 4R7
(506)454-1821

Vancouver Society on Immigrant Women
2425 Cypress Street
Vancouver, British Columbia
V6J 3N2
(604)731-9108

West Coast Domestic Workers' Association
107 - 96 East Broadway
Vancouver, British Columbia
V5T 1V6
(604)875-8431

Windsor Urban Alliance, Women's Committee
480 McDougall Street
Windsor, Ontario
N9A 1L4
(519)254-0151

Notes

Note: All the names in this book have been fictionalized.

Introduction
1. From the ninth interview in this book.
2. From the first interview in this book.
3. Genevieve Leslie, Women at Work, Ontario 1850-1930. Domestic Service in Canada. (Toronto: The Women's Press, 1974), p.95.
4. Ibid., p.99.
5. Ibid., p.99.
6. Ibid., p.99.
7. Frances Henry, "The West Indian Domestic Scheme in Canada," Social & Economic Studies, Vol. 17, No. 1. (March 1968), pp. 83-91.
8. Ibid.
9. Rachel Epstein, "Domestic Workers: The Experience in B.C.," Union Sisters, (Toronto: The Women's Press, 1983),p.223.
10. From the sixth interview in this book.
11. From the fifth interview in this book.
12. Guidelines and Procedures — Foreign Domestic Movement, (Canada Employment and Immigration Commission), Ontario Region Directive, December 16, 1981.
13. Ibid.

Noreen
1. Queen Street; a psychiatric hospital in Toronto.

Molly
1. Without landed status or a work permit.
2. Capital of Jamaica.
3. Upper middle class area of Toronto.
4. The Queen Street Mental Health Centre in Toronto.
5. While on a work permit.

Angel
1. Female conquests.
2. Slum housing — four or five houses on a small plot of land.
3. Withdrawal method.
4. Depo-provera.
5. A chauvinistic term which is used in referring to Eastern Caribbean territories.

Primrose
1. Radio Jamaica Redifusion.
2. Jamaica Broadcasting Corporation.

Irma
1. A mental hospital in Kingston, Jamaica.
2. Slum housing — four or five dwellings on a piece of land.
3. Cornmeal mixed with water to make a batter.

Gail
1. Workers who are not landed have social insurance numbers beginning with nine.
2. Montessori is a method of pre-school education.

Shattering the Silence
1. Statement on Labour's Rights, Ontario Federation of Labour, 1982.
2. The Employment Standards Act, Government of Ontario, Queen's Printer, 1982, p. 43.
3. bid., pp. 48-49.
4. Wages for Housework Movement. This demand was first raised in a speech by Polga Fortunata in Italy in 1974. Quoted in All Work and No Pay: Women, Housework and the Wages Duel, Wendy Edmond and Suzie Fleming, editors, (Bristol: Falling Wall Press, 1975),p. 18.
5. Angela Y. Davis, Women, Race and Class. (New York: Vintage Books, 1983),pp. 237-239.
6. Wayne Roberts, Honest Womanhood (Toronto: New Hogtown Press, 1976), p. 13.
7. Charlotte Perkins Gilman, The Home: Its Work and Influence. (University of Illinois: 1972),p. 52. A reprint of the 1903 edition with an introduction by William O'Neill.
8. Ibid., p.71.
9. From the last interview in this book.
10. Jean Baker Miller, M.D., Toward a New Psychology of Women. (Boston: Beacon Press, 1976), p. 8.
11. Gilman, p. 321.
12. Davis, p. 223.
13. Ibid., p. 223.